Being Church

So thankful for you Polly! We love you!

Thanks for your love. You are a gift!

gretchen miller

Being Church

Jamie Miller

Contributors:

Dan Halvorsen
Sarah Stadler
Gretchen Miller
Scott Clements

Consumed Publishing
Bloomington, Minnesota

Published by Consumed Publishing.

Consumed Publishing is a ministry of Consumed Ministries. Consumed Ministries exists to share, both in words and actions, that Jesus Christ desires to give life to the full. We highly value our relationships with God & people, believing through the context of relationships we can provide the resources, speaking opportunities, and training to effectively lead people into the abundant life Jesus promised.
www.consumedministries.com

Edited by Kristy Nordeen
Cover Artwork by Benjamin Stadler
Cover Layout by Eric Beavers
Interior Design and Layout by Gretchen Miller
Interior Illustrations by Kayla Gisch

Published in Bloomington, MN by Consumed Publishing
Printed in Eagan, MN by Salem Communications

Unless otherwise noted, all Scripture quotations are taken from *The Holy Bible: English Standard Version (ESV)*, Containing the Old and New Testaments, Wheaton, IL: Crossway, 2011 Print.

ISBN: 978-0-9839560-3-7

Library of Congress Control Number: 2016956504

Printed in the United States of America

The Dedication:

Considering this entire project is about the amazing identity of the church, this book can only be dedicated to my wonderful church family I follow Jesus with: The Garden Communities. I dedicate this work to all the GCers, both past and present, along with our friend churches here in the Twin Cities we also share life and mission with...which definitely includes my brother (or father, depending on if you are talking to him or me), Gary, and the New Life Community.

If it were not for all of you, then the text in this book would merely be theological concepts my heart and soul have not yet experienced. Because I am fortunate enough to be the church with you, however, I've experienced the beauty and wonder of God's family. We've laughed often together and you carried me through the difficult journey of grief following my sister Penny's death. We've seen God take our small efforts and initiatives and perform Kingdom-sized transformational stories in people. You've inspired me with your selflessness and courageous faith. More than anything, you made me believe that the church is most definitely everything God said she is, as written by the New Testament authors. Thank you for allowing me to participate in the full life of Jesus! I love you, brothers and sisters!

My heart agrees with Paul when I consider you:

I thank my God every time I remember you. In all my prayers for all of you, I always pray with joy. (Philippians 1:3-4, New International Version)

The Acknowledgements:

It is absolutely impossible to acknowledge everyone that had a part in making this book a reality, but here goes...

Dan, Gretchen, Scott, and Sarah – I will always cherish your sacrifices and participation as co-writers in all of this. There's no way I could have done this without you!

Gretchen – Yes! You get a second mention here. The interior work of the book is magnificent.

Kayla – Thank you for the interior artwork. Your talent and heart are both beautiful!

Ben – Thanks for helping with the cover design and sharing Sarah to this project.

Eric – You do all the little things I hate doing. Thanks brother!

Kristy – You endured four different writers and all our literary quirks. (And Dan thinking this was some kind of competition to see who had the least grammatical errors.) Thank you!

Dunn Brothers Coffee – Most of my portion of this book was written while sipping coffee in one of your fine establishments.

Music – I can't write without music. Specifically, Housefires, Will Reagan, Brad Killman, Charlie Hall, Adele (can't help myself), Coldplay, Dave Matthews, and Tim Reynolds. And, of course, my guitar mentor, Dan Halvorsen.

Dan and Gary – Many of the concepts in this book originated on Thursday mornings. Thank you for being my friends and partners in the Kingdom of God.

Tori, Isabelle, and Macie (Tooey head, Ponsi, and Bubbie) – Every day I serve the church, I am driven by the hope of you continuing to partner with Jesus in growing her beyond the gates of darkness.

The Contents:

The Author:

Jamie Miller

Since the time I was a fetus, I grew up in a church environment. My parents raised me in a home where God was central to everything we did. My parents' greatest desire for my three sisters and me was simply to walk with God all the days of our lives. They weren't too concerned with what career we chose or where we lived as long as we continually strove to seek God's kingdom and His righteousness first. I am who I am today because of this foundation, and I will be eternally grateful for it.

Throughout my middle and high school years, many people in the church I was raised in sensed a call to church leadership for my future. Not only did this scare the mess out of me, I felt in no way compatible with the job description I perceived of a pastor. Throughout college and into my late 20s, this gentle push into church leadership became a forceful shove from God. I knew in my heart, and it was confirmed by many I trusted, that it was time for me to step out with a few like-minded brothers and sisters in God's family to launch a new church. This small band of Jesus' followers began meeting in my living room in 2006 and my life has never been the same since. My love for the beautiful church of Jesus has grown expediently this last decade, because I firmly believe the only way that children of God will experience the abundant life Jesus wants for them is through belonging to a family of God they pursue Christ and His mission with. I have committed my life to growing as many of these communities as I can while God's breath fills my lungs. I wake up every day blessed, thankful, and invigorated to assist willing people into a deeper relationship with Jesus.

I am currently in the beginning years of my 40s and am still learning how to embrace the middle years of life. My best friend and wife is the beautiful Gretchen Miller. I've known her now half of my life and we've been married for 18 of those years. My other housemates include three daughters. They are Tori (15), Isabelle (13), and Macie (9). In these three girls, I see the best of Gretchen and the worst of me (at least that's how it seems to me). It has been a wonderful joy to see them grow up in a church family that loves them almost as much as Gretchen and I do.

I enjoy the following: a cup of coffee or a wonderful meal shared with friends and family; conversations about what God is doing and will do (I am a visionary fella), a fall Saturday afternoon on the couch watching my beloved Ohio State football team play, the sport of basketball (more coaching and less playing these days), a run or the chance to lift some weights, stumbling through a song with my guitar in hand, staring at Gretchen, laughing with my girls, or watching anyone do anything that they truly love.

The Contributors:

Dan Halvorsen

> Jesus and his disciples went on to the villages around Caesarea Philippi. On the way he asked them, "Who do people say I am?" They replied, "Some say John the Baptist; others say Elijah; and still others, one of the prophets." "But what about you?" he asked. "Who do you say I am?" Peter answered, "You are the Messiah." (Mark 8:27-29, NIV)

After this passage, Jesus goes on to teach the disciples a great deal about who He is and what His mission is. In my experience, Jesus' knowledge of these things is rare. Many of us want to know who other people think we are. A much smaller segment of us ask the question of ourselves. Who am I? Writing this bio forced me to ask this very question. Who am I? How can I write about myself in a way that would be meaningful to you, the reader? Like you, I am a culmination of experiences with people, victory, loss, rising, falling, success, tragedy, and God. I'm no different than anyone else in that way. In the same way, each of us is beautifully unique. It's pretty cool to think that you are the only one who possesses the exact recipe for the way you think. It's also pretty cool to think that you were made in God's image and that He chooses to reveal bits and pieces of Himself through you. I happen to believe that God is revealing Himself to you, through me, even now.

Here are some key experiences that developed me into the person I am today. I am pretty familiar with these stories, because I was there. Someday, I hope to hear your story. Actually, I think that's what this book is all about.

Milestone 1: Globe trotting

When I was about seven years old, my dad decided to travel around the circumference of the Earth by land. He did this because God told him to do it. He didn't question it. He just packed his wife and three kids into a car and drove from Minneapolis to New York. We had very little money, so we sold the car in New York and used that money to buy plane tickets to England. A series of curious events took place that resulted in my family traveling the circumference of the world by land. I learned that faith mixed with some good old-fashioned disregard for fear takes you a long way. Literally.

Milestone 2: Realizing I am a weirdo

Because we lived all over the world, my mom homeschooled us kids. Also, due to living all over the world, I didn't exactly have a lot of peer influence in my life. We kids stuck together like a tribe, having developed our own jokes, games, etc. As amazing as this experience was, it also resulted in me becoming a kind of nerd that is difficult to describe. Since this is a book, I'll try to describe it anyway. My favorite outfit was a purple sweat suit that had the face of a wolf on the front. I would tuck my wolf sweatshirt into matching sweatpants. Then, I tucked the pants into some glorious tube socks, accented by off-brand high-tops. I didn't like to change out of this outfit. I pined away while it was in the wash.

During my junior high years, my dad started a church in Ireland. I was able to attend a public school. At this point, a sort of clash of cultures occurred. You see, most people grow up being influenced by the sights, sounds, people, TV shows, and music around them. This causes many folks to gravitate toward a type of social norm. I didn't have any of that going on in my formative years. I had not gravitated toward any kind of norm. My classmates didn't take too fondly to my oddities. I got picked on quite a bit. Sure, this was sad, but after a time I realized that I would not be able to earn respect by following others' rules. I started to make my own rules, becoming more confident in the weirdo that I was. It's amazing how alive you become when you stop trying to be someone else. Through this experience, I discovered a deep love for promoting the uniqueness of others—a love I use in my work to this day.

Milestone 3: Encountering a chronic illness

I found out I am a diabetic at the age of 17. I have attended a lot of prayer services and healing conventions, but I'm still a diabetic. I believe God can heal diseases if He wants to, and I have discovered that He doesn't always heal us when we ask Him. I also believe, really believe, that whatever God does is best.

Milestone 4: Becoming a family man

A big part of who I am is directly due to the influence of my wife, Heather, and my kids, Bjorn and Ingrid. Heather and I have been married 11 years as of writing this. While I'm a big-picture action man, Heather is detailed, efficient, and practical. She rounds me out beautifully. My 5-year-old son Bjorn's name means "bear" in Norwegian. He has the strong personality to suit his name. He's a talker, a natural leader, and he will definitely be a handful when he is a teenager. My 2-year-old daughter, Ingrid, is more the strong, quiet type. She has that stoic Norwegian thing down. I think she is musical and I'm excited to see where that leads. It's hard to know whether my thoughts are my own or some combination of my family's thoughts. This might be the definition of co-dependency, but I like whatever rhythm it is that we have discovered.

Milestone 5: Becoming communal

Almost 10 years ago, my wife and I made a pact with some close friends. We decided to pursue God together, no matter what. We get together frequently and we know each other intimately. I don't know what I'd do without them in my life. This experience opened my mind and heart to the church community, of which my wife, kids and I are now a part. Our church community stresses relationship, even to the point of how we are writing this book. You can grow a certain kind of strong by yourself, but you can grow much stronger with the help of others. It's not always easy, but the end result has formed much of who I am and who I am yet to be.

That's me; right now, at least.

Sarah Stadler

Here we are, just you and me. The reader and the writer. Uninterrupted and alone. Probably one of my favorite kinds of relationship. I blame my introversion on being raised from the very bottom of a stack of siblings. My family taught me very early on that the best way my voice could be heard was one on one. Or to scream over everyone else, but I'm just not naturally that feisty. I'm happy to be here with you and offer a little of my humble biography, even though I would much rather be talking about you.

I am the momma to two children. I start there on purpose because nothing on this mortal planet makes me feel more alive than they and the man who gave them to me. Life as I knew it completely changed the morning I laid eyes on my firstborn son. Although he's not perfect, and neither is his younger sister, I can't stop the love eruption that happens inside me every time I think about them. My husband, Ben, is truly the Yin to my Yang; he and I have been sharing life together for ten years.

I feel a tad bit bolder when I use written words over verbal words. My writing, like nearly everything else in my life, comes from the heart. And releasing my insides out into this great big world is like therapy for my soul. I blog, I dabble in poetry and songwriting, and I published a book of short stories. I also run an in-home business with my mother that has taken up a lot of my time over past five years. I am humbled to say that most of my work flows from delight and leaves me feeling blessed and rewarded.

I've always been drawn to the mystical wonder of spirituality. I never live a day without noticing the presence of God. From as early as I can remember, I've accepted the relationship of depth offered by the Divine. Growing in a clearer understanding of Jesus and embracing His practical teachings as a way of life has been more of a journey for me.

My writing on church stems from the impressions left behind after three decades of development by four different fellowships. Each of them moved me and changed me, bringing me greater questions along with a stronger desire for transformation. When I think back to the seasons I shared with these churches, I see faces and remember the feelings they gave me and everything they taught me through grace and love.

Gretchen Miller

My name is Gretchen. I am the wife to my best friend, Jamie, and mom to three beautifully unique daughters: Tori, Isabelle, and Macie. I am a journal-keeping, vegetable-gardening, mini-van driving, soccer and basketball mom and, on most days, I absolutely love my life. I have been a stay-at-home mom since my oldest daughter was born almost 15 years ago, although I have always worked some sort of part-time job. As the girls have gotten bigger and have begun to spend more time at school and activities and less time at home with me (sigh), God has opened up space for me to do and be involved in some different things. It is a new season, and I enjoy it. For the most part, I feel pretty settled and confident in many of the roles and places God has put me, and I am thankful for that, because it was a process to get here. But, at the same time, I find myself stepping into some new places—places I never dreamed of going. They are stretching me—really stretching me—which I am learning to be thankful for. It keeps life fresh and interesting, or at least that is what I keep telling myself. One of those places is here, collaborating on this book, with some humble thoughts on my life and experience with the church.

In a few months, I will turn 40 years old, and all of those years I have spent as part of a church. My parents are first-generation Christians, meaning that for a long time they were the first and only people in their families to follow after Jesus. They wanted me and my two sisters to know and love God, so they raised us in the church. My family was in attendance at all church functions. So growing up, I participated in vacation Bible school, Sunday school, youth group, and AWANA (an outreach-based program for kids that focused on Scripture memory). When I left my parents' house and married Jamie, we continued to be a part of the local church. We served as Sunday school teachers, nursery workers, and leaders in two different college and young adult groups. When our girls were born, we brought them right into the life of the church, in hopes of continuing to build on the foundation that was built in us by our parents.

Being a part of the church for such a long time, I have seen a lot. Sadly, I have seen, and even been a part of, some days in the church that were not pleasant. In fact, they were downright ugly and hardly reflected the heart of Jesus. But I have also been privileged, thankfully much more frequently than the latter, to see and experience some amazing, life-altering, glimpse-of-heaven moments with the church. These are the days that I live for and hope to foster in my time here on Earth.

When I think about the church, a favorite song normally comes to mind. It was written by Jeremy Riddle and is called, "Prayer for the Church." My favorite refrain says:

> *And now she's shining,*
> *Her light is blinding as she sings your name*
> *And now she's beauty*
> *Up from the ashes, your love is on her face*

These words resonate so much with how I feel about the church. I have seen her beautiful and shining, and I am hopeful God can use me to help her shine the light of Jesus even brighter.

Scott Clements

As we like to say, at the time of this writing:

Gender:	Male
Age:	58 (still officially "middle-aged" by most current definitions, and the elder of this group)
Marital Status:	Married, to Laurie, for 27 years
Children (Human):	Three: a son, age 24; two daughters, ages 22 and 16
Children (Canine):	Two Bernese Mountain Dogs that shed like crazy but lean and love like nobody's business
Education:	Bachelor's Degree from University of Wisconisn-Madison (GO BADGERS!) Master's Degree from Colorado State University (GO RAMS!) Degree of Contempt for Ohio State University (GO JUMP IN THE LAKE, BUCKEYES!)
Religous Background:	Protestant/ United Church of Christ
Occupation by Day:	Construction Manager
Profession by Life:	Procrastinator

I note the "Profession by Life" for the simple fact that this page is the VERY LAST thing I'm writing in our collaborative efforts on this book. It was supposed to be the first assignment. Well, actually the second, after our original response and group meeting, when the whole thing kicked off. We've been done for weeks and Jamie has been hounding me to produce the darn bio. I've put it off, and promised delivery, and put it off some more. Often. Crunch time now, and finally I write.

Delayed not because I don't know what to say, or can't seem to describe myself in a way that makes sense to you, the reader, but because I guess it's just what I do. Jamie will back me up on this, and that's okay. I do know myself well enough to admit my faults (some of them, anyway). So as I reflect on this terrible and pervasive habit at this very late date, I realize that my procrastination has impacted a lot of things in life, including, appropriately, my relationship with faith and God.

I won't tell you here about how I was raised religiously. You will surely, and quickly, get a sense of that in my writings. However, a brief story about my approach to religion as an adult may give you some insight to the confused state in which I live, from the perspective of "church."

I married a nice Jewish girl.

A nice Jewish girl who, sadly, lost both her parents within one year (both from cancer) at the age of 15.

A nice Jewish girl who then moved in with a Protestant family of seven, truly became their 6th kid, and began a life of celebrating both Jewish and Christian holidays. But, quite honestly, she has not attended Temple as long as I've known her (other than weddings, funerals, and bar/bat mitzvahs).

When Laurie and I got together, we had the absolutely brilliant idea of "exposing" our future children to both religions, through Sunday School or whatever, and when the time was right, or the age was achieved, or again, whatever, we'd let them decide "what they wanted to be." You know where this goes.

We have one kid who does not believe in God, one who wished they went the Jewish route (we think simply for the great party and gifts at the mitzvah), and a third who has been confirmed in the Lutheran church on their own accord, first through choir with a friend for the social aspect, which led to Sunday School and so on.

Total abject failure as a parent to provide religious guidance of any kind to my offspring. It's truly the one thing in life that weighs heavy on my mind.

Can I change things? For me? For them? Maybe. I hope so. My stories herein will suggest I'm on a path. I don't know yet where it ends.

The One Thing:

In January of 1998, I started my first semester of graduate school and I quickly realized that my favorite class each semester was the one Dr. Jim King was instructing. Because of this, I tried to take as many classes as I could from Dr. King during my tenure in school. It wasn't as if the other professors were unqualified, uninteresting, or reasonless; I learned much from them as well. I favored Dr. King because he had this way of engaging the students and acquiring their opinions of whatever subject matter was currently being discussed. In Dr. King's classroom, you sensed he was facilitating discourse toward the end he desired. Dr. King never lectured. Actually, most classroom periods he talked the least of anyone in the room. He just asked questions and then just let arrogant, know-it-all graduate students speak.

One of the tools Dr. King used to commence discussion in the classroom was something he called One Thing. During the classroom, whether in the beginning, before a break, or at the end, he would ask everyone in the room to share one thing they've either learned, were still processing, or had additional questions about. The unofficial rules of One Thing were as follows:

1.   Keep it brief. If 30 people were in the class, you couldn't have each person going on and on and on for 5-10 minutes (although there is always that one student that does!).

2.   There is no pressure to come up with something new. If another student shared something you were planning on saying, you could simply say, "I agree with Billy" (assuming you actually agreed with Billy).

3.   Passing is acceptable but not preferred.

During One Thing, I always loved hearing what the other students were taking away from the discussion. One Thing also forced me to think critically about what I was learning and share this information in a clear and concise way.

Over the years, I've adopted the One Thing initiative for my teaching opportunities. When I lead either the teaching time of our church or campus gatherings, I try to leave space for One Thing. As the leader, I always find it rewarding and informative to hear what people are gaining from our interaction. I also think it provides people the space to learn from each other and build vulnerability and honesty among those in the group.

This book is a collaborative effort of five unique writers. For the Introduction and Identity sections, I am the author charged with the duty of providing the content. The other authors read the section I wrote and then composed a One Thing response. After reading my thoughts on the identity of the church and the One Thing responses from Gretchen, Dan, Scott, and Sarah, my hope is that you consume a more holistic cognition of the truth being presented.

I love the approach of this book. You may think I am writing this because I want more people to read it. Well, of course I do! But the honest reason why I love this book is because I know whoever reads it will be learning from five people rather than just one. Naturally, some readers will relate more to Scott, or Sarah, or Gretchen, or Dan, or me. But reading five unique voices will force you to think more critically about what it is you are taking away from all of this and I know you will be better off for it.

You are encouraged to do your own One Thing for each section as well. Saying your One Thing to yourself in the mirror might be a way to accomplish this task. But may I encourage another avenue? Find 3-4 people willing to read this book with you. Commit together to reading a section, then have each person write out his or her own One Thing. Gather the participants together after the responses are composed and have everyone read aloud his or her response individually and let the discourse flow. Who knows? You may even find yourself savoring the experience!

The Back Story:

Have you ever heard what someone said about you that cut right to the tender part of your heart? They make an accusation about you so harmful that it pierces your soul like a sharp knife penetrating soft, fleshy skin. I had that experience recently and, to be quite honest, the words said about me have inspired me to do something I've resisted for several years now... write. I don't view myself as a talented or profound writer. Actually, to be perfectly honest, I don't like to write at all. For me, writing is hard labor. I have friends that enjoy writing. Nothing excites them more than a latte, their laptop, an inspiring playlist, and the pitter-pat of fingers on keys. For me, writing feels more like walking out of my house with one of those gigantic inflatable sumo wrestler costumes on and trying to run a marathon, uphill, with a forceful wind in my face. Oh, and it is raining...hard! For me, writing is a grueling exercise laced with miserable thoughts of hopelessness, despair, and boredom.

Have I painted the picture of my disdain for writing clearly enough? So what statement from someone would motivate me to begin my uphill-in-the-rain-marathon of writing? This statement does: *Jamie hates the church.* A bit of context is in order. My friend Eric visited me recently and shared a conversation he had with my good friends Ray and Lorie Lines. Ray and Lorie have been dear friends to my wife Gretchen and me our entire marriage of 18 years. When we were first married and establishing our new life together in northeast PA, Ray and Lorie invited us over often for dinner. We loved our time in their home. Ray and Lorie will never fully realize how much we learned from them in those early years of marriage. We carefully watched and learned from the way they parented their sons and loved each other. No one I know loves their family more extravagantly than Ray and Lorie Lines! Since those early years of our marriage, God called my family to Minnesota and the Lines' family to Raleigh, NC. This is where Eric lives as well. And this is where the conversation took place in which the inspiring-Jamie-to-write statement was made.

At this fireside chat between Eric, Lisa (Eric's wife), Ray, and Lorie, Ray and Lorie shared with Eric that there is a vacant position of assistant pastor with their church. Ray is on staff as a youth pastor for the church while also working at the US Postal Delivery Service. Ray and Lorie thought this would be a good role for Eric to serve in, so the conversation turned into a recruiting effort by Ray and Lorie to get Eric to consider submitting his resume for the opening. Eric denied the request and then jokingly told Ray and Lorie that I should take the position. Eric fully understands that I am quite happy in Minnesota and believes God has continued work for me here. And then it was uttered. Lorie said, "We can't ask Jamie to consider this position. He hates the church."

When Eric told me this story, something inside of me literally began to hurt. I may have masked it on the outside to Eric, but here I sit 5 days later and am still feeling the residue of that statement. I haven't been able to shake off those horrific words.

I am not upset or angry with Lorie. I love Lorie and understand where she is coming from with making the statement. There are two main reasons why this statement pains me the way it does. First, I actually love the church. I love the church so much God has inspired me to give my life in service to her. Hoping, praying, and believing that my life's efforts will be a part of Jesus' plan of building the church a reality.

Second, Lorie's statement about the church, in essence, captures what so many believe: that the church is simply an organization of programs, buildings, paid leadership positions, and weekly services.

So here I am, typing away on keys in response to that statement. To be clear, I don't hate the church. I actually love the church very dearly. I don't hate programs, buildings, leadership meetings, or weekly services, either. Apparently I've given this impression to Lorie, so I apologize to her for that. I don't hate all of those functions of the church. What I hate is when these functions become so ingrained with the theology of what the church is that the church's growth is stymied into a stand-still position, unable to move forward with the great mission Jesus gave us to do.

I once heard it said by Louie Giglio that "terminology is theology." Basically, what Giglio is saying is that the way we describe aspects of our faith is actually what we believe about them. Specifically, the way we talk about church is a mirror into our actual beliefs about what or who we perceive the church to be. So take a moment and do something for me. If someone asked you, "Who, where, or what is your church?" How would you respond? Whatever your initial response (terminology) may be to those questions is what you actually believe about the church (theology). If our terminology about church is contrary or incomplete with how the Scriptures describe church, then we have some major problems.

The purpose of this book, in essence, is to look at what the Scriptures define as the identity of the church. Because if we, the church, can fully understand our identity, then we will function and grow out of that identity in a Spirit inspired, organic way.

I want to be clear. This book IS NOT a how-to guide for doing church. There are no steps, procedures, or principles laced with acronyms. I will not discuss or critique the various forms of church, either. We will not compare house churches, mega-churches, traditional churches, cell churches, or multi-site churches. God knows there are enough of those books out there.

There are actually thousands upon thousands of books written about the church. This is primarily the reason why I've resisted the occasional urge to share my thoughts in written form. So many have generously given us words of wisdom regarding the church and their books have inspired me. I've recommended them to anyone interested and desirous to grow in their understanding of their identity as a part of God's church. But God recently called to mind what a great man of faith told me after I wrote my first book, <u>Fully Alive</u>. The day the book was published, I received a voicemail from a prophetic voice in my life, John Shumate. His voicemail was concise, but each word was packed with depth and discernment. He said this: "Jamie, your book is not for everyone, but it is for someone." Over the last decade since <u>Fully Alive</u> was written, I've heard from many of those *someones* (pardon my grammar). I am humbled to know God used me to help a few others along with their journey.

I don't know who these *someones* are this time around that God wants His thoughts, expressed through me, to impact. But whoever you are, my prayer is the journey in these pages will unlock for you what was unlocked in my heart several years back about the glorious church of Jesus.

...shall we begin?

The Back Story

The One Thing {Dan}:

…shall we begin?

Jamie's introduction reads to me like a bittersweet love letter to the church. I'm left with a host of feelings and thoughts and I'm excited for a chance to put them out here on paper.

The first question I ask myself is, "Jamie loves the church, but do I?" Take a moment to ask yourself the same question. Do you love the church? It's a deceptively simple question. If you have been a part of the church for any length of time, you know the correct answer. And yet, if you are able to be truly honest with yourself, does that "correct" answer really apply to you? Do you love the church?

My dad is a pastor. Growing up, I was the last to leave church on Sunday and the first to arrive the following Wednesday. On any given Sunday, my dad stood behind a pulpit espousing impassioned diatribes while I sketched on the sheet of paper my mom gave me as an attempt to shut me up. I knew every secret hiding spot in the church building. I knew exactly how many times I could go to the bathroom per service without getting into trouble. I knew how to group-pray in a way that got me a rapturous chorus of "MmmmHmmms" and "Amens" from the people praying with me. I knew what clothes to wear, how to comb my hair, what music to listen to, what political comments to regurgitate, and when to get the ladies' approval by quoting Bible verses. Pardon me for saying so, but I was an expert in church. However, even with all this expertise, I can't deny that I grew up with a gut feeling that church equals obligation. A great example of an obligation is flossing your teeth. You know you should do it. You know it's healthy. But you gotta admit: it's hard to love an obligation.

I have an assumption about love and obligation. I think love is met because our hearts feel for the person on the other end. I think obligations are met because the brain tells the heart to shut up and deal with it. My heart may say, "I don't want to floss my teeth." My brain says, "Shut up and deal with it. It's good for you." Similarly, my heart may say, "I don't really love the church." In those moments, my brain says, "Shut up and deal with it, it's good for you." I'm glad my brain wins in these fights. If not, I'd have rotten teeth and a host of even worse problems.

But what if it doesn't have to be that way? What if I am able to love the church with my heart as well as my brain? What if a world exists where my heart is awakened to the bride of Christ? What if I could anticipate meeting with church the same way I anticipate a hamburger, a great read, or an old friend?

About once a week, my parents would invite this elderly guy over for dinner. I was about twelve years old at the time. He was in his late eighties and had a temper as fierce as a hurricane. While my mom made dinner, it was my job to talk to this guy. It was a total obligation. We didn't have much in common and I would have preferred hanging out with someone my own age. However, as he and I got to know each other, we became friends. He was a photographer and had a fantastic collection of old cameras. He taught me all about selecting film, metering for light, and composing a picture. He had a large collection of pictures that he had taken over his 70-odd years in the hobby. These were fascinating glimpses into a world that existed well before my time. Each picture had a story and some of the stories were quite good. As time progressed, I grew to look forward to our times together. I grew to respect and admire this gentleman for the man I now knew him to be. By the time he died, I considered him as a part of my family. He was no longer an obligation. I say this to make a point about which I am fairly certain. We have to get to know something pretty well before we can say we love it.

Perhaps it is hard for some of us to love the church because we don't really know the church. Maybe we know it as an obligation, as a person we are forced to talk to, but we don't know it as family. Wherever Jamie goes with this book, I'm looking forward to the ride. Perhaps I am the one person for whom this book is being written. Perhaps you are, too.

The One Thing {Sarah}:

If you care at all about the way you come across to people, then you know there's nothing worse than being misunderstood. Especially if you take your gracious status as an image bearer of Christ seriously, a false impression is devastating on so many levels. After reading Jamie's introduction, the part that stuck with me was when he clarified exactly what it was that he hated about the church: *What I hate is when these functions become so ingrained with the theology of what the church is that the church's growth is stymied into a stand-still position, unable to move forward with the great mission Jesus gave us to do.* It's true. It really is immobilizing and painful to witness. I was immediately reminded of one of the saddest misunderstandings I witnessed as a young girl. It didn't make sense to me as a child, but now that I'm older I'm beginning to realize this memory actually runs on a pretty parallel track to my formed feelings about the church. I hope you catch on to how this metaphor connects.

I remember sitting at my bedroom window, watching the movers unload oversized cardboard boxes, wooden bed frames and plush leather furniture. The bright red For Sale sign had finally been removed from the neighbor's overgrown lawn and new life would soon enter the vacant house across our quiet street. After everything was unpacked, the large U-Haul drove away, leaving a clear view into my new neighbor's yard. That's when I saw her. A little girl, just my size, with short brown hair and a dusting of freckles across the bridge of her nose. The willow tree in her new front yard had branches that grazed the ground from months of neglected maintenance. It didn't take her long to gather a handful of boughs and start swinging back and forth with them. I watched silently and smiled to myself. Within what seemed like a moment, she spotted me at my window. I quickly blushed and, before I could even look away, she smiled and waved me over. I stepped nervously across the street as she ran to meet me. It was there, on that warm fall day in the middle of our quiet dead-end street that we met for the first time.

It turned out that she was everything I wanted in a friend. Her joy was contagious, her intuition spot-on. Confident but never overwhelming. Her mind was curious and her body was active. She offered me the feelings of value and excitement that resulted in deep love and trust within my young, growing heart.

I still remember the first time I was invited over to her house to play. It was much different than I expected. Her house's strict rules and rigid guidelines were so limiting. Fake gold picture frames were filled with false smiles. I was so confused; this didn't seem like the place a girl like Jenny would live. I remember having a hard time enjoying her true character within the rigid structure of her home. She just didn't seem like the same girl I knew. Worst of all, Jenny didn't seem happy there.

Sometimes Jenny's face comes to mind when I sit silently on a stiff wooden pew during a church service. I sit there thinking back to the way her mother unintentionally limited her into a *stand-still position*. In the same way, I think about Jesus and the church. I ask myself if we're striving to keep Him in a safe, controlled *stand-still position* or if we are limiting opportunities for His Spirit to move because of our bad habits of focusing energy on things He never asked us to do in the first place.

This introduction makes me rethink a whole lot. It stirs me up and makes me want to learn to delight in valuing the people—who are the church— the way Jesus did and the way I see Jamie doing. The church was originally intended be a place where Jesus' values would be put into practice through us. There's no record that I can find of Jesus practicing anything that disables His followers. I believe His goal through the church is to empower us to continue his work. The Bible gives a marvelous report in Acts about the early church devoting themselves to Christ's teachings and lifestyle, valuing people and relationships above all, practicing repentance and change, gathering together for prayer, witnessing wonders of healing and restoration, accepting the mystery of all that is God, and doing all this while engaging freely and fully with the Holy Spirit. This doesn't sound like a *functional stand-still* to me. This sounds like a call into action!

It's pretty easy for me to fall in love with the church based on common vision and united respect for the One who started it so many years ago. A church where the heartbeat is so strong, character so passionate, and spirits so lively that no terminology can contain it.

The One Thing {Gretchen}:

If you didn't already catch it, I am married to the author of this book. Nineteen years of marriage to someone, especially when that someone is as passionate a person as Jamie, will have a way of making a mark on you. Some of his passions have become loves of mine, like Ohio State football and enjoying a good meal around the table with friends. And some of those passions I have let him enjoy all his own, like the Cleveland Browns, a good cup of coffee, and lifting weights. And while some may think his greatest influence on me has been my love of Ohio State football, it would probably rank second to his influence on my love for the church.

In the course of our life and marriage, there are certain phrases I have heard repeated over and over. The quote from Louis Giglio, "Terminology is theology," is definitely one of those phrases and is the first thing that stands out to me from this section. Admittedly, the first several times Jamie spoke this to me, I was skeptical. I am a defensive person by nature and argued that regardless of what was spoken about "going to church," everyone knew what was meant—the difference was just words, semantics, so we shouldn't overthink it. Time would tell that I would have to eat my words on this one, especially when my kids came into the picture.

Being a parent is easily the most life-changing role I have been given, and parenting made me think very carefully about how I represented the truth of the church to my girls. I couldn't tell them the church was the "Lord's House," because then they thought that was the place that He lived. And I need to be careful about saying we are going to worship in a sanctuary, because I don't want them to think they are off the hook for worship in our home and at their school, too. I don't want my girls to view the church as a service or the place they go to meet God, so I have had to change the way that I speak. Making some small changes, like saying we are going to the "church building" or that "the church is coming over" has hopefully had an effect on the way my girls view the church; I know it has had a personal effect on me. When I choose to speak of the church as people and not as a service or a building, it reminds me that all of life is sacred and that I carry responsibility as part of the church. I represent Jesus and His church in the building, at the service, AND in my neighborhood, in my home, and on the sideline of a ball game.

God has brought me into some new places in my life. Many of these new places put me in the middle of people who have not grown up in the church. They do not come with the same knowledge or foundation that I have been given. They are babies, at best, in their spiritual development. My words need to make sense and, more importantly, they need to accurately represent the truth about the church. I need to say what I mean and mean what I say, because people I care about are listening and taking note.

The second thing that stands out from this section is this: *What I hate is when these functions become so ingrained with the theology of what the church is that the church's growth is stymied into a stand-still position, unable to move forward with the great mission Jesus gave us to do.* This quote reminds me of when one of my daughters first started playing basketball. She would come down on offense and go to the corner and stand there. Her teammate would dribble down the court. My daughter would just stay put, right where she was, not moving. She did not look like she was expecting the ball to come to her, and if it did, I am not sure she would have even known what she was supposed to do with it except to give it back to the one girl that would shoot. This was their only play. My daughter was only a body on the court and had very little, if anything, to do with the offensive plan of the team. As a parent, it was frustrating; she wasn't putting into practice anything she was learning about basketball. She was fully capable of getting involved in the team's plan to win the game, but she didn't know how to, outside of standing in her spot during the play. Her team would have been far more effective if all 5 players were involved in the offense, as opposed to just one, but my daughter was standing still; she was not a contributor. [Disclaimer: she was obeying her coach, but that is a whole other topic of discussion].

I share that little illustration to say, I don't want to just be a body taking up space in the mission of Christ. I want to be a playmaker. If I am in my neighborhood and my neighbor opens up about a health struggle or a marriage crisis, I don't want my only play to be getting them to my church service or into the Women's Bible study that I am participating in. The truth of the matter for me is that many of the people I meet are not interested in coming to a service. A lot of people seem to carry baggage or preconceived notions of who or what they need to be when it comes to entering the doors of a church building. So if all I know is how to get them there, I am not going to be very effective and people will not hear about the great news of Jesus. I am learning that there needs to be more than one "play" to bring people into the life of Christ. Maybe as a member of the church and someone whose life God has changed, I need to start with my own story. I can testify to the work that Christ has done. I have been poured into and discipled, so when the situation arises, I can do it. And while I am doing this, I can ask the church to support me in prayer or even come alongside for the process. I think I have made it far more complicated than it needs to be at times. I am looking for someone else to shoot when God is telling me, "You are wide open!"

The One Thing {Scott}:

church /CHerCH/ noun 1. A building used for public Christian worship.

If you Google the "definition of church," which I did, since I'm not well-versed in the words and practices of religion, you'll find that the World Wide Web can deliver about 133 <u>million</u> results in 0.34 seconds. Quite overwhelming, especially to someone like me, who's agreed to share my thoughts on church with Jamie, Gretchen, Sarah, and Dan. Four people who I believe—at this point in time anyway—to be well into the journey that Jamie speaks of in his introduction. A journey that I'm not sure I've even begun.

For me growing up, church was pretty much as defined above by Merriam-Webster: a place that I had to go to every Sunday. From preschool age, where it really was just daycare with a story time that included characters of unusual names, on to many years of Sunday School and through High School and Confirmation, whereupon I was finally set free by my parents. They, acknowledging my new status as an adult, gave me the choice to attend or not. I chose "not" with the exception of special events: Christmas (including the all-important annual Christmas Pageant), Easter, weddings, and, sadly more frequently in recent years, funerals.

Church was then further reinforced to be nothing more than a building by one of those burned-in memories from my youth. I took off the first semester of my junior year in college to stay home, work, and figure out my career path. The work, as an Assistant Janitor at the Glenview Community Church, was at the very same place I'd been confirmed just a few short years before. My boss was not the Minister, who had so kindly offered me the job, but Carl, a crusty and cranky old guy with a my-way-or-the-highway attitude about exactly how everything should be done. One morning, while vacuuming the altar under the cross in the stained-glass sunlight, Carl came racing up the aisle, screaming, "No, no, no, Scott! Wrong, you dumb #*%!, Wrong, wrong, wrong!" He grabbed the vacuum from my hands and yelled, "Not like that"—he gestured to my generally north-south pattern—"Like THIS"—he gestured to his generally east-west pattern. He added, with vigor, "You're #*%!-ing it all up!" Dumbfounded, I cried, "Carl, you can't talk like that. This is a church!" His reaction? "It's not my #*%!-ing church!" I lost something then and don't think I've looked at the place the same way ever since. To this day, that scene plays through my mind each time I attend service there.

I suspected there was much more to it when I first read about Jamie's pain in having someone think that he hated the church. I believe that Jamie has a deep and profound love of Christ and for all people. He cares equally for those he shares his faith with and those who haven't quite gotten there yet. I've come to know this through the patience he's shown with me as I've tentatively stepped in and out of my search for faith. I see that his love for others, for church, is not bound by walls or schedules or budgets, rules and bylaws.

In retrospect, I realize that maybe Carl had it right. It was just a building, and—though a properly vacuumed one at that—Carl knew, as does Jamie, that church is not what HOLDS people, it IS the people.

I guess I can say "I get it" now. Not that I'm buying in just yet. Only that I understand church to be much more than a PLACE of worship. But for the time being, I'm still a member of the Church of the Not So Sure. I suppose that's a contradiction to another definition of church as "a body of religious believers," but I'm confident there's a whole host of others like me on this Earth.

So, as we begin…

I'm a *someone* on the outside, looking in. I'm not sure what I'll find, but I am willing to listen and learn.

The Identities:

church

(noun) \\'chərch\\:

1. called out ones

Some of my friends and family stumble with their words when speaking with me about the church. I am told they are "scared they will say the wrong thing." I guess I have earned a certain reputation about my preferred terminology when it comes to church.

Now I must admit that I've been labeled a bit of a crazy man because I have trained my children to say things like:

"Is the church coming over tonight?" (Usual way to say this: "Do we have church tonight?")

"Where is the church gathering tonight?" (Usual way to say this: "Where is church tonight?")

"What time is the church gathering?" (Usual way to say this: "What time is church?")

"Are we going to so-and-so's church building?" (Usual way to say this: "Are we going to so-and-so's church?")

I promise…my intention is not to raise weird kids (although this may be unavoidable since they have my genes). In the introduction, I mentioned the quote by Louie Giglio that has stuck with me through the years, "Terminology is theology." Basically this statement declares that how we say things is really what we believe about them. So if we ask, "What time is church?" we are implying that church is a service. If we ask, "Where is church?" we are saying that church is a building or location. You may think I am overreaching here, but I do not believe so.

I've had people ask me some of these church questions and I do my best to answer in a way that describes the church in a biblically accurate way. For instance, when I meet a student at Normandale Community College and we begin having a conversation, eventually they ask me, "Where do you work?" I am quite positive this question is asked because they want to know why this 40-year-old guy they are talking to is hanging out at a community college. For many complex reasons, this is a difficult answer to give someone I just met. So I generally say something like, "I am one of the leaders of my church." Nine times out of ten, this is the next question, "Oh…where is it?" I know what they mean. They are asking me where the church facility is that my church meets in. Then, nine times out of ten, I respond by saying, "Well…my church is in Bloomington and Richfield primarily, but we also are in St. Louis Park, Lakeville, and Prior Lake." At this point, they become even more confused! Maybe they think I am part of a mega church that has several campuses. I describe more clearly to my new potential friend that my church does not own a property; we meet in homes or rent other facilities. I tell them that when Scriptures refer to "the church," it speaks of people. Therefore, my church community lives in Bloomington, Richfield, St. Louis Park, etc. Depending on the person's availability and curiosity, a much longer conversation can take place with additional inquisitive questions.

Where it All Began

The first time we find the word *church* used in the New Testament is in Matthew's Gospel, Chapter 16. The conversation starts with Jesus asking the disciples whom people were saying He was. Since many believed Jesus was a prophet, they informed Jesus that some claimed He was Elijah, or Jeremiah, or John the Baptist. Jesus moved the conversation to a more personal matter when He followed up His general question with a particular one for them, "But who do you say I am?" Peter's response is priceless, "You are the Christ, the son of the living God."

This was an amazing answer! So much so that Jesus helped Peter understand how fortunate he was to see so accurately whom Jesus was by saying, "Blessed are you, Simon [Peter]! For flesh and blood has not revealed this to you, but my father in heaven." I bet Peter felt satisfied in that moment and possibly somewhat relieved to have passed the test. Jesus continues by saying, "And I tell you, you are Peter, and on this rock I will build my *church*, and the gates of hell shall not prevail against it."

There we have it! Jesus spoke the word *church* in the New Testament for the first time. It was more of a declaration, actually. Jesus promised that HE would build the church. And nothing would stand in the way of the church's expansion. Not even hell itself will stop this movement of God!

I promise not to bore you with a bunch of Greek words, but in this instance, I feel it to be valuable. The Greek word for *church* is *ekklesia*. This is not a made up word by Jesus. It is a word the culture in that day was aware of. The Blue Letter Bible defines *ekklesia* as "a gathering of citizens called out from their homes into some public place, an assembly." *Ekklesia* is a compound word made up from the two words *ek*--out of, from, by, away from--and *kaleo*--to call, to invite. In its most basic, stripped down language, *ekklesia* means "called out from."

In Greek culture, when a group of people, lets say public servants, left their homes to assemble, their gathering would be called an *ekklesia*. It describes both the called out people and the assembling of these called-out ones.

The New Testament writers took the word and put the emphasis more on the "called out people" definition as opposed to the "assembling" (although the people obviously assembled). Here are some examples:

"And great fear came upon the whole **church** and upon all who heard of these things." – **Acts 5:11**

"So the **church** throughout all Judea and Galilee and Samaria had peace and was being built up." – **Acts 9:31**

"The report of this came to the ears of the **church** in Jerusalem, and they sent Barnabas to Antioch." – **Acts 11:22**

"And when they arrived and gathered the **church** together, they declared all that God had done with them, and how he had opened a door of faith to the Gentiles." – **Acts 14:27**

"Pay careful attention to yourselves and to all the flock, in which the Holy Spirit has made you overseers, to care for the **church** of God, which he obtained with his own blood." – **Acts 20:28**

"…who risked their necks for my life, to whom not only I give thanks but all the **church**es of the Gentiles give thanks as well." – **Romans 16:4**

So where does that leave us? What is the identity of the church? The identity of the church, by using the Biblical word *church*, is really this: the church is people. More specifically, the church is **called out people.**

Called out of What to What

Stay with me here. If the church is made up of many "called out people," then this infers we are called out of something and into something else, right? Better yet, we are called out of something and into something much greater and more complete than what we were once a part of. Let's look at a few examples.

Bondage to Freedom

"I didn't know I was a slave until I found out I couldn't do the things I wanted." - Fredrick Douglass

This is a powerful quote by the famous African-American ex-slave, Frederick Douglass. When I read it, I was reminded of this truth in a spiritual sense regarding sin and freedom from sin. Paul wrote this in Romans 6:17-18:

> But thanks be to God, that you who were **once slaves of sin** have become obedient from the heart to the standard of teaching to which you were committed, and, having been **set free from sin**, have become slaves of righteousness.

We, the called out people of the church, have been set free from the bondage of sin and the shame and guilt our sin brings. Before our belief in Jesus as Lord and Savior, we were bound by the grip of sin. But now, we are called out of slavery from sin and into freedom.

Many in my church family have been blessed to have plumbing work done on our houses, by a man we will call "Charles". Charles is probably the most upbeat, friendly, sweet, and kind man of Jesus you will ever meet. His vocation is plumbing. His mission is plumbing. His life is plumbing. As he told me, "I am a plumber for Jesus."

One evening, as Charles and I were working on a bathroom installation at my house, he shared his life story with me. Charles had fallen into drug addiction in college and for several years was a slave to that addiction. He tried at various times to stop the addiction, but nothing seemed to provide the freedom he desired.

One night, as he lay stoned on the couch, he heard a TV evangelist share the good news of Jesus. In that moment, Charles fell to his knees and gave his life to Jesus as his Lord and Savior. Immediately, Charles was called out of slavery and into freedom. As a called-out person, Charles presently is free from addiction and walking in the freedom only our great God could provide. This is the life we are all called to. We are totally free from sin!

Death to Life

God, in all His creative wonder, designed the first human from the dust of the ground. What I wouldn't give to somehow watch that amazing action go down! There was this first man, Adam, created and fashioned, lying on the ground. There was only one slight problem. Adam was dead! There was absolutely no life in him. But the life-giving God changed all that. The writer of Genesis penned these words in Genesis 2:7:

> Then the Lord God formed the man of dust from the ground and *breathed into his nostrils the breath of life, and the man became a living creature.*

Only the life-giving, all-powerful God could breathe life into a dead body!

Now let's fast-forward several thousand years in human existence to John 11. In this chapter, we find Jesus standing outside of his friend Lazarus' tomb. Lazarus has been dead for a few days now. Standing with Jesus in this scene were people, all mourning and distraught over this untimely death. Included in all of this grieving is Lazarus' sisters, Mary and Martha. But Jesus, with all of the authority and power over death in his hands, looks at that tomb and proclaims, "Lazarus, come out." And, wouldn't you know it, Lazarus came walking out of the tomb. Death to life!

Moments before this miraculous work of Jesus, He made a bold proclamation regarding His identity. John recorded Jesus' words when He told Martha outside of her brother's tomb, "I am the resurrection and the life" (John 11:25). Jesus, in this statement, is claiming total dominion and authority over death.

Only God has the power to take something that is dead and make it alive. This is what He has done for us, the called-out people. He has called us out of death and into life.

Paul reassured this to the called-out people of Ephesus. In Ephesians 2:4-5, he told them this truth through his writing:

> But God, being rich in mercy, because of the great love with which he loved us, even when **we were dead** in our trespasses, **made us alive** together with Christ—by grace you have been saved.

We once were dead in our sins and we were dead spiritually. We once were also dead in our separation from God as Father. BUT…now we have been called out of death and called into life! We are alive in Christ. We are alive spiritually. We are alive to know God as Father through our adoption as His sons and daughters!

Darkness to Light

The darkest place I've ever been is the first apartment Gretchen and I had as newlyweds. "The Cave" as we affectionately called it was a basement apartment in a house located on top of a mountain in Clarks Summit, PA. We loved The Cave and many special memories were made there as a couple of young kids trying to figure out this thing called marriage.

The only window in the apartment was an egress window in the bedroom. If the door to the bedroom was closed, you literally could not see your hand in front of your face in the living room and kitchen of The Cave. This made Sunday afternoon naps sublime and they would last much longer than needed.

The only downside to this amazing sleeping environment was the unexpected booby traps Gretchen would unintentionally leave out for me (at least she claims it was unintentional) in the living room as I tried to make it to the light switch. On more than one occasion, I would stub my toe on boots, books, or other random belonging of hers that she would leave out in the middle of the floor, causing me physical pain and harm.

The Cave, and memories of aching toes, reminds me of this--harmful and bad things lurk in the darkness. Satan, the enemy of God, lurks in the darkness. Evil lurks in the darkness. The world system of today lurks in the darkness. And before our faith in Jesus, you and I were a part of this darkness.

But now, we are called out of darkness and called into light. Jesus tells us this very truth:

> You are the light of the world. A city set on a hill cannot be hidden. Nor do people light a lamp and put it under a basket, but on a stand, and it gives light to all in the house. In the same way, let your light shine before others, so that they may see your good works and give glory to your Father who is in heaven. (Matthew 5:14-16)

This is a fairly simple truth to understand, but the ramifications are extremely powerful. Because if we, the church, have been called out of darkness and into light, then light shines in the darkness every place our feet take us. When my brothers and sisters in Christ and I enter Normandale Community College, the campus now has the light of Christ. The same goes for my neighborhood, Anytime Fitness, bleachers at an athletic event, and wherever else we, the called-out people of God, go. We bring the light of Jesus into the dark spaces. Remember--Jesus said He would build His church and the gates of hell (darkness) will not stand against it!

Called from Selfishness to Selflessness

"Who are you thinking about right now?" This is a question I have asked my daughters a minimum of 500 times over the years. I learned this question from my college coach, Mike Show, because he would ask us this question a lot during the course of a long season. I ask my daughters the question when I sense they are oblivious to the other people in the room, desiring to have only their needs met. Typically, I am asking the question because their sweet mother is running around with her hair on fire serving everyone and instead of stopping for a second to consider what she is doing, they will ask her for more mustard, or a ride to a friend's house, or that they need more money for the latest school project or field trip.

I know that the real reason I get so upset with my daughters is because I see my own selfishness in their actions. By nature, we are selfish creatures. From the time we are little infants, we sit around and think about what we want to make our lives a bit more complete.

The twelve men Jesus shared His life with were pretty selfish as well. A few times in the Gospel writings, we find these men arguing over who the greatest is or who will be sitting next to Jesus in the Kingdom. But in one display of servanthood, Jesus demonstrates with actions the importance of being called out of selfishness and into selflessness.

In John's Gospel, Chapter 13, we read of Jesus and his followers sharing a final meal together before His imminent arrest, trials, beatings, and execution. For the sake of impact, I am going to write this one more time. In John 13, we read of a last meal shared together between Jesus and His disciples before His arrest, trials, beatings, and execution! Jesus obviously had a lot on his mind! If there was ever an excuse for self-centeredness, Jesus possessed that excuse during that meal.

Yet, Jesus took that opportunity to display the life we've been called into. Humbling Himself to the lowest of classes, He takes a basin with water and a towel and begins to wash the disciples' feet. Jesus washed the disciples' dirty, grimy, and smelly feet. And when He finished doing that, He told them to go and do the same for those around them.

Jesus showed them that the life of a called-out person is selflessness. We've been called out of a life of pleasing ourselves and into a life of serving humanity.

Many people who live this kind of called out life inspire me. They are always the last ones in the meal line. They sacrifice their time and money for friends and neighbors in need. They wait on widows. They adopt the children no one else wants. This is the life of a called-out person. This is the life of the church.

Called Into Jesus' Life

I could write page after page of "called out of and called into" scenarios. But I think it is best to summarize all of these by simply writing that, at the core of this called-out life, we are called into the life of Jesus. In every conversation, every choice, every action, and every thought, we live the life Jesus would live if He were inside of our skin. This is the called-out life. This is who we are. As Paul wrote in Galatians 2:20:

> I have been crucified with Christ. It is no longer I who live, but Christ who lives in me. And the life I now live in the flesh I live by faith in the Son of God, who loved me and gave himself for me.

So who is the church? Well, hopefully we've learned the church isn't something you do, but an identity to live out. The church is you and the church is me! The church is people called out of bondage, death, darkness and selfishness and into freedom, life, light, and selflessness. The church is people who've decided that investing their lives into the areas Jesus values is the greatest life they can live. Does this describe you?

Called Out Ones

The One Thing {Dan}:

From death to life, from darkness to light...

I tend to think of a word as an empty chalice. It can be filled with whatever meaning I dictate. For example, think of the phrase, "bless her heart." In Minnesota this is a phrase of endearment. In North Carolina, this is a derogatory phrase. The words are the same, but there is meaning behind the words that supersedes the words themselves. As another example, think about how Richard Prior talked about racism. Prior used language that would have been completely offensive if we didn't understand he was making a point that superseded his words. The idea behind the word supersedes the word itself.

With this as my belief system, I struggled to be excited about a chapter that proposes that terminology is theology. Many dull drafts of this response ensued. On some days, I was determined to make my response work, and on others, I was ready to throw in the towel. This bout of mental wrestling (or just plain being mental) finally led me to a conclusion. I'm proud to announce that I did not throw in the towel after all.

I naturally make snap judgments based on intuition. After a time, I realized that I had made a snap judgment of this chapter because of the first section. Unlike me, you probably realized that what follows the first section is an acknowledgment that we are called out of yucky stuff and into yummy stuff. And yet, I missed a lot of that because I was hung up on a quote that I didn't like. When I finally read Jamie's section on being called from selfishness to selflessness for the sixth time, I was struck by how dead I had been to this chapter. I wasn't focusing on life, light, or being selfless. In fact, I gave myself a great case study in the contrast of the life Jamie is writing about.

Death to life

Jamie writes about how God's breath brought life to Adam. As one who is "called out," my breath should bring life, too. Can I do that while focusing on what I dislike? I think not. I'm currently asking myself: how many times do I operate out of a death mentality? Once I figure it out, I'll add my answer to this section of the book. Until that time, I bet it's more than I would care to admit.

Darkness to light

Jamie writes that we are called from darkness into light. When I think of darkness, I think of the unknown. In total darkness, our senses are reduced by 20%. We are less capable of knowing our surroundings. Being unaware is another form of darkness. When I am unaware of something, I often say, "I was in the dark," or, "I was kept in the dark." I think part of being called into light is being called into a heightened awareness.

Case in point, Paul says, "We destroy arguments and every lofty opinion raised against the knowledge of God, and take every thought captive to obey Christ." I think Paul is painting an example of living in light through heightened awareness. Can I live the way Paul is describing if I am "in the dark" when it comes to areas where I fail to submit to Christ in my thinking? Probably not.

This "unaware" type of darkness creeps into life nearly every day. It's similar to reading by a well-lit window in the living room. After a few chapters, you realize that the sun has set, it's really dark, and you can barely make out the words on the page. You are surprised that you didn't notice the setting sun earlier. I think this is another reason why doing church is more beneficial when it is done alongside other folks. They can point out the fact that the sun has set before you will notice it for yourself.

Selfish to selfless

I have covered the fact that I didn't enjoy this chapter the first five times I read it. But then I had to ask myself Jamie's question, "Who are you thinking about right now?"

When I focus on what I dislike, I am often focused on *my* dislike. This is a self-centered way of thinking. After contemplation, I realized that a less self-centered option is to focus on what I agree with and what I want to encourage. We will never agree on every point, but we can agree on many points. I want the points of agreement to be the area of my focus. Think of the last fight you had with a loved one. It becomes so easy to focus on that one thing on which you disagree, forgetting the myriad of things on which you are in total agreement. When I think of being called to a life of selflessness, I think of a life that is called toward agreement.

This chapter has reminded me to:
- Focus my thoughts and language on life-giving topics
- Keep darkness at bay by taking every thought captive
- Be selfless in my thinking by focusing on the areas in which I am in agreement

The One Thing {Sarah}:

As I read this chapter, I began to ask myself the same question that Jamie is asking you: is this revolutionary exchange of callings visible in my life? In this section, Jamie takes us through four bullet-point examples of what we are called out of and into as followers of Jesus. The bullet points left me with a great deal of introspection and made me question how seriously I take Jesus' calling for me and my church community to be different from the lifestyle of the world.

I began asking myself: Do I embrace the freedom I've been called into? Does my view on church seem constricted and binding? Am I seeing resurrection, change and newness in myself and others in my church fellowship? Does the light that I've been called into and the light of my church offer hope and blessing to others or does it blind others? Does the church I'm a part of operate with an inward focus or an outward focus?

There have been times in my faith journey where I've felt *pulled out* and other times where I've felt *called out*. The older I get, the more I realize how many of my interactions with God are hinged on my heart condition. There are definitely times God feels a little more controlling and discerning. Other times, God seems very hands-off and far more interested in a call-and-response kind of relationship. Both are done in love, both are practiced often, and both are used as a tool to cultivate trust in my wondering human heart. I have tasted God's deliverance and can recall many experiences where it felt as if I was being pulled out of one place and brought to safety and peace in another. Through those experiences, God has definitely proven to have the character of a good father to me. So much so that I have a vivid reoccurring dream of large masculine hands lowering down to rescue me out of trouble as they slowly close in around me. It's kind of like the little green aliens who lived in the arcade game at Pizza Planet in the *Toy Story* movie, waiting for the heavy metal claw to drop down and save them.

I assume we have all felt like a helpless toy alien at some point in our lives, right? I must say, though, that as much as I relate to, dream of, and love a

God who pulls me out, there is also something very attractive about a God who extends an invitation to me. It creates the feeling of responsibility and expectation that births dignity within my soul. I, like many of you, respond better to an invitation into something—one where I'm given an opportunity to respond to God and the calling—instead of depending on deliverance offered by God to come pull me out.

It is possible for the church to be made up of relationships with God and others, instead of dictatorship by God over others. During different seasons of my life, I've witnessed both. One of them called me into love and growth, while the other paralyzed me in fear.

As a parent, when I witness my two young children hear and accept the call from a lifestyle that binds them into a life lived freely, I can't help but celebrate. When I see them willingly take part in life-giving activities without me having to convince them it's good for them, I rejoice. When they shine their light for others to see, instead of hiding in the darkness, I can hardly contain my joy. When one of them chooses to be humble and selfless to build up the other, I see the kingdom of heaven at work. God has called them out and they have answered. They are no longer powerless, waiting for a superhero or metal claw to come pull them out. They are empowered and engaged in relationship with the Almighty by responding to the invitational call to follow Christ and be the church.

I could share a personal story about each one of these calling examples we have been given. Bondage to freedom, death to life, darkness into light, selfishness to selflessness; I've experienced them all! However, I am only one small part of the church. Consider the many other followers of Jesus as well. *We* are the church; *we* are the people group who needs to make these polar opposite examples our identity! I believe when we do, those who are resisting the call, remaining in bondage, death, darkness and selfishness, will see Jesus through the church. Being Jesus' witnesses is all we've been asked to do! What a difference responding to the call can make.

The One Thing {Gretchen}:

In this section, I find myself reflecting on what Jamie calls the "extremely powerful ramifications of a fairly simple truth": Jesus called me the light of the world.

Churched or unchurched growing up, most people have heard the song "This Little Light of Mine." You know, the one where you hold your pointer finger up in the air and you sway with the chorus of people proclaiming you will, "Let it shine, let it shine, let it shine." And, in my church growing up, we had a couple more verses to this song. Maybe not as well known, but my personal childhood favorites were, "Hide it under a bushel? NO! I'm going to let it shine," and, "Don't let Satan [blowing sound] it out; I'm going to let it shine."

I am definitely not blaming the song, but as I think about my light in the world, I often think of it as fragile—a small candle whose flickering little flame needs protection or is at risk of getting snuffed out because I covered it up. But now, I wonder if my mindset was too protective, too defensive, and I have underestimated the power of Jesus calling me—calling all of us Jesus-followers—the light of the world. Because it matters how powerfully we view ourselves. Not because of who we are, but because of who makes us light. The light of Jesus in us has power to overcome the darkness in our world and we don't need to be afraid to let it shine.

As I consider these truths, I have a new vision for my light. I am upgrading my little candle flame, a light that seems to only flicker in dark places, where evil lurks and Satan thinks he owns the place. I'm upgrading from a candle to a sparkler, a never-ending sparkler, that doesn't just flicker, it shines. And it not only shines, but it shoots light into the blackest of black, in a display that inspires awe and wonder to children (and even still to this adult). Its light is powerful and it can make an impact on the darkness. My light is powerful and it can make an impact on the darkness.

And even greater than my light being powerful is this: I am trading your candle—our collective candles as the church—the tiny flickers that we have protected and defended or that we have considered powerless against the evil of the world. And in my mind, I am joining us together like two sparklers connecting. You know that moment—the moment when as a child you light one sparkler by joining it to another—and the light flashes so bright you think it will burn you. This is the kind of light that I believe the church can bring to the world's darkness. This is me and you, together as the church, advancing the Kingdom of God's heavenly light against the kingdom of darkness and, according to Jesus, the gates of hell don't stand a chance. What a powerful truth. So, sparklers up!

"Let it shine 'til Jesus comes. We're going to let it shine, let it shine, let it shine."

The One Thing {Scott}:

So here I am, that guy on the outside looking in, and now all I can think is, contrary to a comment in my response to Jamie's Introduction, "I guess I really <u>don't</u> get it."

The instructions we received from Jamie at the beginning of this journey were to *pick one thing* and write a personal reaction to his comments, rather than write in an effort to teach you, the reader. That's pretty easy, because religion falls far outside my area of expertise or experience, and *I'm no teacher.*

It's now been pretty well established herein that the church is more People and less Place or Thing (what was that game—20 Questions?). If there's a whole darn book being written by the five of us travelers, there has to be something even deeper inside our discussion, or the whole story can be wrapped up by these first two short chapters. In the closing paragraphs of Jamie's reflections on the called-out ones, he writes, "This is the called-out life. <u>This is who we are.</u>"

Well…here's my one thing. As I see it, Jamie has written the whole story, so far at least, with the perspective or expectation that all of our readers ARE called-out ones. Those who might just need to fine-tune their carburetors: the mix of air (their life) and fuel (their faith) that makes them run smooth, strong, and righteous. Me? I probably need a full engine overhaul.

I admire and respect those of you who have seen that light and have been "called out." I—evidently, admittedly, and realistically—am not one of them. Nor do I even know how to join the club. I just don't understand how or why it happens to some and not others, not me.

I remember hitchhiking back to Madison on a dark night after a weekend home from college. Vividly, because it was brutally cold outside. After a lot of time spent on the shoulder of I-94, I was lucky to finally find myself in a warm van. I'd snagged a ride with a guy at a gas station west of Milwaukee and, with just under an hour's worth of drive time ahead, he engaged me in some serious theological discussions. I recall being "all in" with the rather lively conversation, but when we stopped at the Capitol Square to say our goodbyes, my 50-minute friend turned to me and asked, "Are you ready right now to take Christ into your life as your Lord and Savior?" I'm thinking, "Seriously?" And all I could say was, "Are you freaking kidding me?"

Fast-forward 30-some years, and along comes Jamie's "Charles the Plumber." Lying on the couch, stoned to the bone. Likely with orange-crusted fingers jammed into a bag of Cheetos. Some TV preacher dude (I'd actually like to know who it was) putting on his Big Show, and BAM! Right then and there, Charles gets hit square in the head with the everlasting love of Jesus. That's all it took? Sounds way too easy for me.

What am I doing wrong? I'm a pretty good guy, or so I'm told. Far from perfect, though we all know that nobody is. Certainly not criminal or even heading that direction by any stretch of the imagination. I haven't smoked pot in years. C'mon, Charles, what's your secret?

In Jamie's closing sentences, he declares, "The church is people who've decided that investing their lives into the areas Jesus values is the greatest life they can live." He asks, "Does this describe you?"

I think it's obvious. For me, the answer right now is no. But I wonder if that can be amended to "not yet."

I guess I sometimes feel like, in this crazy-busy life I lead, I simply don't have time for God. What scares the crap out of me is that feeling this way could very well result in God not having time for me.

church
(noun) \\'chərch\\:

2. body of Christ

hef's Table is a Netflix documentary series featuring the premier chefs we have on this planet. Each episode offers a fascinating look into some of the most eclectic people alive, their exquisite culinary skills, and fabulous restaurants. If you decide to give the series a try, I highly recommend not watching the shows while hungry. The close ups of amazing, mouth watering food while your stomach is growling does not aide in self-restraint and dieting!

Massimo Bottura, an Italian man in the city of Modena, Italy is the featured chef in episode one. My wife and I greatly enjoyed the passionate demeanor of Massimo and, since we love Italian food, we were immediately hooked.

Chef Bottura's restaurant in Modena, Osteria Francescana, was voted the third best restaurant in the world by San Pellegrino's World's 50 Best Restaurants in 2014. It was clearly evident during the episode that the restaurant has been an integral part of the life of Chef Bottura and his wife, Lara Gilmore. Osteria Francescana is more than a place of employment for Bottura. The restaurant is intertwined with his entire life, including his family.

Lara Gilmore jokingly points out during the episode that Bottura even proposed to her on the same day he opened Osteria Francescana. She says it was his way of saying, "Do you want to marry a restaurant?"

She goes on to say, "The restaurant has always been our family, and a big family. My kids grew up celebrating big birthdays at Osteria Francescana. My son Charlie has this sense of love in the restaurant where lots of people are around who care about him and want him to have fun. I love that! The fact that the restaurant was our home and we lived just down the street.

And when it was closing time we were there and between services (we were there). And you know...it is our baby."

Massimo Bottura ends the episode with these words (imagine hearing them in an Italian accent), "If you have a success. If you live an incredible moment of happiness, that happiness is much, much more deep and big if you share it with others. And you get to that point together. It is like the happiness and the feeling is exploding...it's double. This is the point."

Life is never meant to be lived in isolation. Chef Bottura realizes this. All of his many accomplishments as a chef are doubled because his awards and innovative cooking style are shared with his family and restaurant staff. This includes his entire staff—from the glamorous position of Sous Chef down to the entry-level position of dishwasher. So when his restaurant, Osteria Francescana, is voted the third best restaurant in the world, the enjoyment is much fuller because he shares the accolades with the people he loves and lives his life and dreams with.

A Full Life

Jesus proclaimed in the Gospel of John, "I came that they may have life and have it abundantly" (John 10:10). I am convinced that we will never experience the fullness in life that Jesus desires for us outside of His church, however. Chef Bottura describes the happiness experienced with others in his restaurant as a feeling of explosion. Paul writes something similar to the church in Ephesus. He wrote to those early saints that a full and abundant life is only experienced within the relational parameters of the church. Specifically, this is what he writes:

> And God placed all things under his [Jesus'] feet and appointed him to be head over everything for the church, which is his body, the fullness of him who fills everything in every way. (Ephesians 1:22-23, NIV)

Let's not brush too quickly past these modifying phrases. God appointed Jesus to be *head over everything for the church*. But then there is a comma inserted. The phrase that comes after the comma is the description Paul gives for what the church is. Paul wrote that God appointed Jesus to be *head over everything for the church, which is His body*. Paul describes the church as Jesus' body.

Another way of saying it is this: *The church is the body of Christ*.

And then, after Paul describes the church as the body of Christ, we find another comma. Stay with me! I find commas to be very entertaining! This next phrase, after the second comma, is a descriptive phrase about the body of Christ. Paul wrote, *which is his body (the church), the fullness of him who fills everything in every way*. The fullness of Jesus is manifested in the body of Christ, which is the church. You see, if you desire to be full of Jesus, then you must be fully immersed in Jesus' church. The fullness doesn't happen any other way. We are filled with Jesus through our relationship with the church, which is His body.

One Body, Many Parts

If we are honest here, this is a little strange at face value. What does it mean that the church is the body of Christ? If the church is the body of Christ, then what part of His body am I? Am I an eye, or the liver, or a toe? Hopefully I am not an armpit!

In Paul's epistle to the church in Corinth, he tells them:

> Now you [the *you* here is plural] are a part of the body of Christ, and each one of you is a part of it. (1 Corinthians 12:27, NIV)

He also writes:

> Just as a body, though one, has many parts, but all its many parts form one body, so it is with Christ. (1 Corinthians 12:12, NIV)

As persons, you and I are individual parts of the body of Christ, which is the church. Paul, in 1 Corinthians 12, continues the physical metaphor by describing some parts of the body: some like an ear and others like an eye. We are valuable as a part of the body but isolated from the rest of our parts. We are incomplete. We need each other to live, function, breathe, and perform the works desired of God.

Back to Ephesians 1—Paul wrote that the body of Christ (the church... in case you forgot) is *the fullness of him (Jesus) who fills everything in every way.* Unfortunately, I run into so many brothers and sisters in Christ that tell me they feel distant from God. They do not know the fullness of Christ Paul describes in Ephesians 1. So I ask them who the brothers and sisters in Christ they are walking out their faith with are. I always get this general response, "I don't have anyone like that in my life." They are breathing and living this Christian life in solidarity. Some may attend a Sunday service. Some may even be registered on a church's membership role. But they are not actively engaged and attached to other people pursuing Christ and His mission. And since this lack of participation with the body of Christ is not a reality for them, their lives are void of the fullness of Christ.

These people are like an eyeball just bouncing around the world, detached from the human body. How goofy would that be! The eyeball can see but cannot hear, cannot speak, cannot walk, cannot touch, cannot smell. An eyeball is an amazing part of the human body, but I am glad I have more parts to my body than just my eyes. I enjoy the fullness that seeing, hearing, touching, smelling, and tasting brings.

The body of Christ I pursue Christ with is very diverse. We have introverts and extroverts. We have parents and children. We have men and women. We have white Americans and people raised in other countries and cultures. We have people with Baptist backgrounds, Catholic backgrounds, and Pentecostal backgrounds. We have people that have followed God for many years, some who are just beginning to follow Jesus, and a few that are trying to figure out if following Jesus is something they want to really do with their lives. We have teachers who love to be out in front of people with the spotlight shining brightly upon them and we have servants perfectly content to be behind the scenes where no one notices. We have people that love watching sports and those that think the only parts of the Super

Bowl worth viewing are the halftime shows or commercials. We are many members, but we are ONE body. We have various talents and abilities, but when used in conjunction with one another, a beautiful and fuller expression of Christ is manifested.

My life without this body would be void of completeness and meaning. I need the other parts of this body to bring my relationship with Christ into abundance.

The Head

> Speaking the truth in love, we are to grow up in every way into him who is the head, into Christ, from whom the whole body, joined and held together by every joint with which it is equipped, when each part is working properly, makes the body grow so that it builds itself up in love. (Ephesians 4:15-16)

I love these verses because they allow me to take a big, deep sigh of relief. I am not in control of the body of Christ, because Jesus is. The church is His body and He is the head! He is the one holding everyone and everything together. Sometimes I run myself ragged trying to hold everyone and everything together and, as soon as I realize how incapable I am of doing this and relinquish this responsibility into the hands of Jesus, I experience such relief.

I hear my friends get asked this question from time to time, "Do you go to Jamie's church?" This question is very troubling to me! Since I am one of the leaders of my church, people talk of the church I share my life with as if it is mine. I understand where they are coming from, but my church is not *my* church (Jamie's church). My church is Jesus' church. Jamie is not the head of the church; Jesus is! Jesus is the one building His church, not Jamie!

Trust me, you don't want me as the head of the church. I do have responsibilities in the life of my church. I do have my part to play. I lead, train, and equip the other parts of the body to walk with Jesus and serve humanity. But only Jesus can sustain and hold all of us, His body, together.

I am not a doctor nor do I claim to be, but I do realize a few basic aspects of the human body. For instance, I know that if the rest of my body is detached from my head, I will not live for very long. I think we can all agree on this profound biological truth I so eloquently proclaimed.

As silly as this may read, I think those of us that claim to be a part of the body of Christ forget how vital it is for us to remain attached to the head, our loving savior, Jesus Christ. To put it very bluntly and succinctly, NO CHRIST = NO CHURCH. You can gather people one day a week, sing some songs, have a nice talk from the front, socialize throughout the week, do a kids' program, etc., but if Jesus is not pursued, proclaimed, and followed as a collective unit, then you may have a religious club, but you do not have His church.

I wonder if your church, the body of Christ, is attached to Jesus. I pray it is. If you are looking for a church to immerse yourself in, I pray you find one that is *growing up in every way into him who is the head, into Christ*. If and when you find such a collection of eyes, ears, hands, and feet, I know the full life of Jesus will be experienced in your journey in new and profound ways.

The Beautiful Face of Jesus

Each spring, my church participates in a retreat together. We've found these times to be foundational to the life and health of our community. This past spring, we were at a camp near Lake Mille Lacs in central Minnesota. Although our spring retreat is usually the second weekend in April, our "spring" retreats usually feel more like a winter retreat here in Minnesota. Typically, we are hiking around in snow boots and winter jackets, as the days of blustery winter conditions are in its final stages. But this year was different. The snow was melted and on the Saturday of the retreat we actually jumped above 70 degrees. We were outside the entire day, enjoying the beauty of God's creation together.

After dinner, we gathered for a group photo. Since we were already outside, it was suggested by one of our leaders that we hold our worship through singing by the lake rather than in the Log Inn. So we did! Those of us that played guitar were jamming away as the kids sang and danced before the Lord. This was one of the most worshipful moments of my life.

The final song we sang to Jesus was "You're Beautiful," by Phil Wickham. The lyrics of the song pointed my heart to the greatness and beauty of our wonderful God. As we sang the final words together, I turned around to play my guitar and sing while looking at the sun setting on the opposite side of the lake. We sang this line over and over and over again, *I see Your face, You're beautiful, You're beautiful, You're beautiful.* The streaks of various shades of orange and red in the sky were breathtaking as they touched down upon the water. The wonder of God manifested more as the sun inched closer to the lake.

But then, in the midst of singing *I see your face, You're beautiful,* I turned around. In that moment, I saw an even greater vision of beauty that went well beyond the extravagant sun and body of water. I saw the beautiful face of Jesus in Ben, Sarah, Jeremiah, and Lydia. I saw the face of Jesus in Dan, Heather, Bjorn, and Ingrid (Inga). I saw the face of Jesus in Dan, Heidi, Evelyn, Anna, and Reise. I saw the face of Jesus in Danny, Megan, Tanner, Ashley, Marissa, Sonia, Gary, Minh, Erin, Nick, and Sergio. And, of course, I saw the beautiful face of Jesus in Gretchen, Tori, Isabelle, and Macie. The face of Jesus that night was amazingly gorgeous. Actually, this wasn't just the face of Jesus. It was the body of Jesus. The body of Jesus I share my life and mission with.

This body has made my life so complete, so full, and so overflowing that I am blessed beyond belief. And to the head of this body, the great and powerful King Jesus, I worship and adore. Being a part of this body is the point—Chef Bottura is definitely right!

Body of Christ

The One Thing {Dan}:

For me, the thing that really sticks out about this chapter is the fact that Jamie finds commas entertaining. I imagine Jamie looking at commas and giggling. It makes me laugh, but it doesn't really make for a great response. So, I must move on to other thoughts. Speaking of which:

> "Our happiness is much, much more deep and big, if we share it with others…"

For some reason, I started thinking of the Marlboro Man while reading this chapter. If I'm dating myself too much with my Marlboro Man reference, you can substitute Don Draper from *Mad Men* for the same effect. I think a lot of us, maybe especially men, want to be like the Marlboro Man. He's so strong that he doesn't need anyone or anything. He lives on the side of a rugged mountain, smoking his rugged cigarette, and riding his rugged horse. He seems content and, even if he weren't, you'd never know because he is so stoic. Come hell or high water, he stands alone and he's just fine with that. I asked my wife if this ideal appeals to her in the same way it appeals to me. She thinks the average woman doesn't want to look like the Marlboro Man, *per se*, but she agrees that women share this idealism. As an example, Instagram is flooded with profiles of the perfect mom. She looks amazing—no hair is out of place. She is artistic. She is a great cook, and her house is perfectly curated. She needs no one.

Try to imagine the Marlboro Man at a *Chef's Table*-style dinner. He looks across Chef Bottura's table and sees only his horse. What a lonely existence! Maybe the Marlboro Man's life is only glamorous when put on a billboard and viewed from a distance. Maybe, beneath the facade, he's just a lonely guy with a lot of regret about trading a life with people for a life with that dang horse. No wonder he smokes so much. He's trying to end it all as quickly as possible!

But, I think I have fallen prey to the Marlboro Man's hollow dream. Let's say it is Sunday morning. I turn to you and say, "Pick a church building."

We walk in to see what it is all about. The place is filled with well-dressed, happy looking people. A service occurs. After the homily, people get up, make a few pleasantries, flood the local diner, and leave without tipping (at least according to my friends in the food industry). We join in. After lunch, we go home and life continues. Maybe we repeat this experience 52 times a year for the rest of our lives. Thirty years later, we've certainly attended a lot of services. But, have we missed out on something more meaningful?

Maybe you are thinking, "What could be more meaningful than being in church on Sunday?" Even some of my friends that aren't part of a church tell me they think they should be in a church building on Sunday, or at least their kids should.

Here's what I'm getting at—Jamie wrote about seeing the beautiful face of Jesus as he sang with his community. When I think about his experience, I realize that Jamie had to take a moment to notice the faces of those with whom he was worshipping Christ. He looked at the faces of his fellow worshipers in order to see Christ's beauty. I don't do this much. Maybe I never do this, which begs the question, "Why?" Maybe it's because I, like the Marlboro Man, don't think I need others.

That's what really resonates with me about this chapter. It is a farce to think I can be like the Marlboro Man while also being the body of Christ. It's as much a farce as an eyeball thinking it doesn't need an optic nerve. In order to experience Jesus, I need my brothers and sisters. I want to see the beautiful face of Jesus in those around me.

Regardless of how cool the Marlboro Man looks from his billboard, I want to avoid that empty kind of existence. I want to be thankful that I need other people, and that I can see Jesus in other people. To paraphrase Chef Bottura, I want my happiness to be much, much more deep and big because I share it with others. Though, to be honest, I wouldn't mind looking as cool as the Marlboro Man while I do it.

The One Thing {Sarah}:

This section was a challenge for me to respond to at first. The team and I received this section via email last week. I read it right away and began trying to form some simple initial thoughts. This mental haze could be due in part to the fact that both my children were up multiple times the last few nights. Their quiet whimpers and sweaty brows made it hard for me to settle into my normal subconscious state of rest. Throughout the night, their need for a mother to come alongside and offer alleviation to their discomfort was so frequent that I decided to spend what remained of the night in the living room close by their bedrooms. I made a place for myself to sleep on our cold leather couch, under two drafty windows that were failing miserably to keep the Minnesota winter winds out. I tried to make warmth by snuggling under an old blanket that my grandmother knit, but even still, it didn't take long for the discomfort to kick in. I missed my king-sized bed downstairs and the furnace of a husband with whom I share it. But there, in the living room, during the dead of night, something about the idea of the body of Christ clicked inside my mind.

I realize now that the needy children, restless sleep and a cold couch were all part of the sifting process to bring to the surface a clearer understanding of how the body of Christ could work as separate members coming together, serving as one. There is nothing within me that would ever wish a disconnect from my children, even when they are suffering. Solidarity kicks into high gear, causing me to enter into the crisis right alongside them every single time.

The next morning, with a hot cup of coffee in hand, I spent some time researching exactly what it may have been that Paul was getting at with the metaphorical image in his letter to the Ephesians. I felt like a breakthrough happened the night before and hoped that my research would solidify the experience I had and the understanding that was beginning to form. Sure enough, there it was, in the very same verse; the pairing word to "body" happened to be "joint." A connecting piece: the part of a structure that binds together separate pieces that were originally scattered. Joints are typically not glorified body parts in today's world, but after taking a minute to consider their purpose, I found that what was once a blurred metaphor began to take focus within my mind. These words came to mind: touch, connect, unite, serve, strengthen, empower, cooperate, commit, tie, fasten, bond. I want to offer these verbs to the church I'm a part of. But how?

Last year, a young couple in our church welcomed their first baby. After Megan's full term and flawless pregnancy, we were all shocked to find out her sweet new baby was unable to breath on his own after delivery. Medical staff rushed in to offer aid to the fading child. They performed vigorous CPR for six minutes straight before the baby boy was able to take his first weak breath. The doctors knew that, after being deprived from oxygen for that amount of time, something needed to be done to slow the possible swelling that could happen in his tiny brain. Baby Lucas needed to undergo hypothermia treatment immediately. Megan watched helplessly, unable to hold her newborn as he laid alone, shaking, on a cooling blanket for 72 hours. After three days of therapy, the time had come to slowly begin to warm up Lucas. This process would take 24 hours of gradual temperature rising under close medical supervision. We, Megan and Danny's close friends and active body of Christ, were unwilling to simply stand by and wait to hear the results. This was an opportunity for us to practice living as supporting joints in the body of Christ and that is exactly what we did. We connected ourselves to them in every way possible: through prayer, meals, gifts, visits, texts, and love. We were the joints that served and strengthened. We were working as a unified group. We touched, connected, united, empowered, cooperated, committed, tied, fastened, bonded and displayed the great love of Jesus to the world and each other. Baby Lucas' body responded to the therapy just as the doctors had hoped, recovering without any permanent damage. He immediately bonded himself, full of trust, to his parents. As we bonded ourselves, full of trust, to God.

When I'm hungry, I eat something healthy. When I'm tired, I sleep. If I have a headache, I do whatever I can to relieve the tension. I am highly in tune with what my body needs and have learned to take good care of it. When it comes to my kids, I accept their pain as if it were my very own. I'm really good at taking care of them as well. This leaves me asking myself,

"What do I need to do to keep myself in the place where this is true for the church that God has called me into partnership with? How can I take better care of the body of Christ?" I want to be a joint that can be depended on, one that serves the structure well. I want to be fully connected to the overall function and design of what the church was created to demonstrate to the world.

The One Thing {Gretchen}:

I echo Jamie's sentiment at the end of this chapter: I love dearly the body of Christ that we follow Jesus with; they make life full, and I feel very blessed. But, what I keep thinking about from this section is this: Why do we choose to isolate ourselves from the rest of the body in the first place? Because I have spent time doing just that as well.

The easy answer would be we just didn't know. We didn't know the sweetness, the fullness, is found in being connected to the body of Christ. We didn't know we function more effectively as a part of a whole, rather than just a part. We didn't know, like Massimo, that, "This is the point." And that may be some of it. But, the truer answer, at least for me, was this: While I knew what the Bible said, and I thought I could trust Jesus—the perfect, flawless, holy, head of the church—I did not know if I could really trust people—the less than perfect, flawed, but sometimes holier-than-thou, parts of His church.

I was sitting with a dear friend recently; she has known me for a very long time. As we were chatting about our early years of friendship, she made the comment, "You were really private back then, so I didn't know what was going on with you." It was a true statement. In fact, when Jamie and I first started dating, someone warned him against dating me, because they called me a "fortress"—an impenetrable person. You could say I have been a goofy eyeball, out bouncing around by myself. Part of me was being "strong." I could do it. I didn't need help. I was capable and not a "weak link." And the other part of me was afraid, insecure, and unsure about how the rest of the body would respond if they really saw my imperfections and weaknesses. I didn't want them to judge me, be disappointed in me, or worst-case scenario, cut me off from the body. This may sound ridiculous to you, but I have seen it happen. I think sometimes people in the church view the body as a well-oiled machine—defective parts not welcome. Sadly, I have spent days in my Christian experience viewing it that way, too. Yikes, scary.

There isn't really space to go into what changed all that in my life. Suffice it to say, growth is a process. Most of it had to do with resolving who I am in Christ. I AM weak, but He makes me strong. My weakness doesn't make me incapable, but rather recognizing I need Jesus and His body makes me capable of receiving the strength He wants to display in me. The rest had to do with the beautiful people, including that dear friend, who so graciously modeled the love of Jesus to me by allowing me to be imperfect while at the same time encouraging me to grow more like Christ and be the best part of the whole I could be. The beautiful body showed me the love and fullness of Christ, and it really did multiply the joys of life and ease the weight of life's burdens.

So, today, I am thankful for a lesson learned but also challenged to be a part of the body that best represents Jesus, the head, to my other parts. I do not want to cut off, isolate, or shame parts of the body that are hurting, broken, or just fearful. I want to aid in healing, restoration, confidence, and growth. I really do need you, and you really do need me. And we all really, really need Jesus. I love that this is how He designed it to be.

The One Thing {Scott}:

SCOTT

IS

CONFUSED

I wrote nothing else. Zip. Nada. Zilch.

Upon receipt of Jamie's section, I thought to myself, "This time I'm going to get right on it." No more waiting for last minute inspiration, which has been my usual mode of creative writing and a habit formed long before I was ever requested to participate in this current literary adventure.

So I opened the file, printed a copy, and read. And…nothing. I put it down for a week (maybe two), then read it again. And again…nothing. Now, in each of the four days leading up to "the gathering," I read again, in earnest. You know what I got.

I showed up at the Miller's with one blank sheet of paper (for show), another page simply stating, "SCOTT IS CONFUSED," Jamie's manuscript with my various notes, thoughts, and comments I'd written in the margins during my efforts to "pick one thing," and a thought that I would listen to and question Gretchen, Dan, and Sarah on their essays. My hope was to find clarity—something that had eluded me thus far—in the words of others.

Perhaps this was cheating in a way. After all, we had been challenged to offer a personal reaction, and all I came up with was that same old refrain: *I don't get it.* Assuming their work has preceded mine in this particular chapter, you've felt the powerful emotions of their responses. Leaning on them to get me through this roadblock made me feel like I was letting the team down.

I'd picked up on several particular sentences and paragraphs in Jamie's words:

I read, "A full and abundant life is only experienced within the relational parameters of the church."

I heard, "YOU CAN ONLY HAVE A FULL LIFE IF YOU'RE PART OF A CHURCH."

I read, "This lack of participation with the body of Christ is not a reality for them…their lives are void of fullness."

I heard, "YOU ARE CONDEMNED TO A LESS THAN JOYFUL LIFE UNLESS YOU GIVE YOURSELF COMPLETELY TO THE CHURCH."

I read, "If you desire to be full of Jesus, then you must be fully immersed in Jesus' church."

I heard, "YOU'RE EITHER ALL IN OR ALL OUT."

And I asked, "How do you KNOW if you desire to be full of Jesus?" It occurred to me that Charles the Plumber probably didn't know of his desire. He was just lying on that couch in a smoky haze, satiated with Cheetos, and BAM.

The answers came.

Jamie pointed out that Charles didn't necessarily go "all in" that day, but he had finally turned a corner in his life.

Gretchen suggested to me that we are all on a path, and we are most certainly all at very different places on that path.

Dan drew the path—a simple horizontal line—with *Bad Life* on one end and *Good Life* on the other and *Jesus* somewhere in the middle. He felt that every individual can choose which direction to go, and that most of us have traveled each way at some time during our lives, but a choice to follow Jesus down the path is surely bringing you closer to the good life and grace of God.

And Sarah, bless her, said she believed I was a lot farther down that good path than I may have thought.

So there it was, in front of me, with me, surrounding me...that one thing: "I need the other parts of this body to bring my relationship with Christ into abundance."

My heart warms.

church
(noun) \\'chərch\\:

3. family of God

The first Sunday of each month, my church community has a Celebration Gathering. All of our community groups come together. A few months ago during a Celebration Gathering, we had some visitors join us from Normandale Community College. One of these visitors was Amal, a classmate of Coco's, the student who currently lives with my family. To fulfill one of the assignments for her Psychology of Religion and Spirituality Class, Amal came to our gathering. Everyone in this class, as part of their course experience, had to attend three religious services or festivities and then write a report on what they observed during their participation. I asked Amal if I could read her report, because I am always curious about what people think after they visit any of our church's gatherings or functions. Coco said Amal was nervous to share her thoughts with me, but she granted me favor and emailed me the report a few days later.

I was very humbled and pleased to read the report and realize the kind of effect our church had on Amal that evening. I am going to share part of this report with you. In the report, Coco is referred to by her full name, Nicole.

Over the weekend Nicole graciously welcomed me into her home, where she has church at. I was beyond nervous about going to Nicole's house because it's basically going to someone's home to observe their religious beliefs. Attending anyone's house for the first time is intimidating in general but to attend when you really don't know them and just basically watch what they do. I really didn't know what to expect going, the only thing I knew was Nicole was Christian and that her church was in her house or it moved from house to house. I thought that they would talk about certain topics maybe something in the bible or share stories. Before going over her house I personally thought I knew a lot about Christianity and the basics about their religion. There was a brief moment where I was worried about how people would react towards seeing a non- Christian with a head scarf coming to their home while they are trying to worship, it was a little nerve racking. Another thought I had before going was that maybe there weren't that many people that attended or that they gather together after going to a church at like a facility of some kind. Aside from my thoughts and concerns I was really excited to see something different. Usually when I hear church I think of a huge building with a cross on top and just different visuals.

When I pulled up to Nicole's house there were a lot of cars outside I thought to myself are all these people inside her house that made me a little bit more scared. Once inside Nicole introduced to everybody, they all said hello and seemed nice. There were people sitting in what I think was a den where they were playing guitar and singing. Nicole explained to me that they were practicing and run down of how the evening usually goes. Looking around I noticed there were so many different people some kids from Normandale that were a brought by a friend so it was their first time coming as well. Nicole mentioned how usually there isn't this many people but today they combined both communities together for a celebration that they usually have once every so often.

Shortly after everyone gathered around and sat together for music, which I think was my favorite part of everything I saw. Kids sat in the center and everyone sang along with the music, they also wrote a song to a friend of theirs who was away. As I was listening to them sing I think to me personally this was an awe moment, I just got this warm feeling. It was like you could almost feel the passion and love they all had for their religion. The singing would sometimes get louder and at times I would catch myself smiling because of how genuine that moment looked. This wasn't your typical church that I have heard of or would see on television where everyone sits and listens as one person speaks, I felt here everyone was together as one.

Jamie went through a passage and went into explaining it more and would engage everyone to speak up and say something. I liked how everyone has the chance to speak or talk where it feels like they are all equal in a way. Two people talked about how their lives have been in the past few months and the religion part of it. I found that part really nice for them to share bits of their lives and everyone really looked like they cared. Personally I feel like you don't really see that much in religious places, seems like people just go to go or that they might need something and want to pray.

They continued into other things we all split up and they prayed for things they were thankful for and give a little prayer to the group leaders because they needed help with a decision they were making. I didn't speak up during the prayer, but I did send a prayer that I hope they do get what they are asking for. Regardless of the fact we come from two different beliefs always sending good prayers or wishing them good things is just the human thing to do.

Once everyone was done praying and talking we headed out for dinner Jamie invited me which was so kind of him to do when he doesn't know me at all. Kindness like that or generosity like I think is just basic human things, but I also think it was connected to his religious beliefs as well.

I overall had a great experience going to Nicole's home the family friendly environment they have was mind blowing. I was really touched by how nice everyone was and devoted they were to their beliefs. If you are someone who has a belief in something or nothing I believe you would been really touched by watching this family like church. You get this feeling of calm and peace with a sense of love and care that I really don't think you see in many places whether it is a place of worship or anywhere else.

My purpose in sharing this story is most certainly not to boast about my church. Trust me, there are many times we've had visitors and blown it royally. I share the story rather because the observation of Amal is exactly what I would hope any person would say once they've observed the relationships my church has with one another. Amal saw us as *family*. She sensed there is a genuine love and care we have for one another and I can honestly say this is a true statement. In my church, we love each other like brothers and sisters should. Do we drive each other crazy at times? Absolutely! Do we fight? Definitely! Are there disagreements and conflicts? Without question! But every family has these struggles. What makes us family is that we love each other, pursue Christ, and strive to stay together no matter what.

The Family of God

The church is the *family of God*. We are brothers and sisters with the same Heavenly Father. Some of us are spiritual fathers and mothers to younger saints in the faith, while being the sons and daughters to those fathers and mothers that are further along in the faith than we are.

This is not my original idea! Jesus, the Son of God, sees the church as God's family, too. He refers to His fellow disciples as *brothers and sisters*. In Jesus' longest recorded teaching in Matthew 5-7, He uses the word *brother* 8 times. When told His mother and siblings wanted to speak with Him, Jesus responded by saying:

> For whoever does the will of my Father in heaven is my **brother** and **sister** and **mother.** (Matthew 12:50)

While teaching his disciples how to pray, Jesus said, "'Pray then like this: Our **Father** in Heaven' (Matthew 6:90)."

Jesus wanted those disciples to know that God is their Father and they could address him as such.

Here are other Scriptures that speak to the church as family (all emphasis is mine):

> But to all who did receive him [Jesus], who believed in his name, he gave the right to become *children of God*, who were born, not of blood nor of the will of the flesh nor of the will of man, but of God. (John 1:12-13)

> In love he predestined us for *adoption as sons* through Jesus Christ, according to the purpose of his will. (Ephesians 1:4b-5)

> Do not rebuke an older man but encourage him as you would a *father*, younger men as *brothers*, older women as *mothers*, younger women as *sisters*, in all purity. (1 Timothy 5:1-2)

> For all who are led by the Spirit of God are *sons of God*. For you did not receive the spirit of slavery to fall back into fear, but you have received the Spirit of *adoption as sons*, by whom we cry, *"Abba!*

Father!" The Spirit himself bears witness with our spirit that we are *children of God*, and if *children*, then heirs—heirs of God and fellow heirs with Christ, provided we suffer with him in order that we may also be glorified with him. (Romans 8:14-17)

Think about this list: *children of God, adoption as sons, father, brothers, mothers, sisters, sons of God, Abba Father.* All of these descriptive names elicit the idea of family. Jesus shed His blood on the cross so we could enter into a relationship with God as our Father. When we enter into that relationship with God as Father, we also inherit brothers and sisters as well. We become a part of the largest family in the world. Ethnicity, nationalities, social and economical lines do not separate this family, because we all have one Father!

The Problem with Dysfunctional Families

Jesus describes heaven as *my Father's house* in John 14. This is an amazing analogy that I can relate to easily. In 1968, my parents bought a home in the Riverbend neighborhood of Columbus, Ohio. Twelve years later, I was born. I spent my entire childhood growing up in that same house with two amazing parents and three other moms, also known as my sisters. When I graduated from high school, I moved to Pennsylvania for college and ended up living among the Pocono Mountains for eleven years. The first four years, I attended college; the final seven years, I was a young married man and the father of two little girls. In 2004, my family moved to the Twin Cities in Minnesota and we have been here ever since. All of this time, however, my parents have lived in the same two-story house in the west side of Columbus.

Because of the distance from Minnesota to Ohio and our increasing responsibilities as a family, my trips to Ohio have become less frequent recently. But when I do have the opportunity to travel the 790 miles from Bloomington, Minnesota, to Columbus, Ohio, I always love making that final turn on to my parents' street and shortly thereafter pulling into the driveway of the house filled with a plethora of stories.

There isn't a place in the house or on the property where some kind of memory hasn't been made. I can go into the family room and recall where countless hours of Buckeye games were passionately viewed. During the holidays, I can see the familiar decorations and remember all the past Christmases celebrated with siblings, parents, grandparents, and adopted grandparents. I can look at the driveway and remember the basketball hoop that allowed literally thousands of games (and a handful of fights) to be played with neighborhood friends. I can walk into the kitchen and think of the Texas fudge cakes, graham cracker crumb pies, and M&M cookies my mom made. I can walk downstairs to my dad's office and remember times when he would sit behind his desk and I would sit on the couch with our dog, Pete Rose Miller, as we conversed about all kinds of world affairs.

When I think of that house, the great memories are not of the structural building itself, but the people that live there currently, have lived there in the past, and the thousands of people that have been hosted inside those walls. The family within the house makes that house a home! I treasure that house because the family I was blessed with that lived in that house generally modeled (no one is perfect) how God desires His family to function.

I know the experiences I had in my home are not typical for everyone. When Jesus metaphorically refers to heaven as the house of our Father, there are those of us in His family that cringe.

I often remind my church that we are a family. A few months ago, after telling one of the ladies in our church for the 796th time (probably felt that way to her) that church is family, I realized that in her mind this wasn't necessarily a positive identity for the church. She spent her childhood bouncing back and forth in between two houses because of divorce. In each house, she strived to live up to the expectation each home placed upon her. She also felt the squeeze from the parent she wasn't currently with to make sure equal time was distributed between both homes. Although her family is made up of good people, her family sometimes caused feelings of stress, unfulfilled expectations, and disappointment. So when I referred to the church as *family,* she thought, "Oh, no. Here is another group of people I have to juggle into my chaotic life and another parent to please—even though I probably won't be able to do so." Her view of family was broken, so therefore her view of the church as family was broken, too. Maybe some of you can relate to my friend as well. If so, I want to remind you of a few truths about the church family.

GOD IS A GOOD FATHER

You're a Good, Good Father
It's who you are, it's who you are, it's who you are
And I'm loved by you
It's who I am, it's who I am, it's who I am

Cause you are perfect in all of your ways
You are perfect in all of your ways
You are perfect in all of your ways to us

This song was written by Anthony Brown and Pat Barrett. I literally heard the lyrics to this song for the first time the exact moment I began to write this section. I don't believe in coincidences. Seriously, this kind of stuff only happens with God! He was reminding me through Pat Barrett's singing that He is a good Father. Actually, He is the greatest father we could ever have! He is perfect in all of His ways and that includes his treatment of us, His children.

Read what Jesus says about our Father:

> Or which one of you, if his son asks him for bread, will give him a stone? Or if he asks for a fish, will give him a serpent? If you then, who are evil, know how to give good gifts to your children, how much more will your Father who is in heaven give good things to those who ask him! (Matthew 7:9-11)

Using the parable of the prodigal son, Jesus describes our Father this way:

> And he arose and came to his father. But while he was still a long way off, his father saw him and felt compassion, and ran and embraced

him and kissed him. And the son said to him, 'Father, I have sinned against heaven and before you. I am no longer worthy to be called your son.' But the father said to his servants, 'Bring quickly the best robe, and put it on him, and put a ring on his hand, and shoes on his feet. And bring the fattened calf and kill it, and let us eat and celebrate. For this my son was dead, and is alive again; he was lost, and is found.' And they began to celebrate. (Luke 15:20-24)

Jesus tells us that our Father knows what we need and is willing to provide exactly what we need if we will simply ask Him. He is also the kind of Father that is always ready to welcome us back when we wander away from Him. And as Jesus' story proclaims, He not only welcomes us back—He throws a big old party and celebrates because His lost son or daughter has returned. I am blessed to have a dad that loves Jesus and loves me. He is a great earthly father. As I was growing up in his home, my dad invested in me, provided for me, pushed me to dream big, worked hard to provide me the opportunities to have successes, and he supported me in everything. He rarely missed my football, baseball, or basketball games, concerts, or big events. To this day I know I can count on him to do whatever I may ask or need of him.

Some of you reading this can't relate to my fortunate upbringing. You didn't have that kind of dad. So when I write of God being our Father, the baggage of your childhood is somehow dragged into the picture. For you, God as Father becomes a tainted image. Brothers and sisters, our Heavenly Father is a good Father! Even the greatest earthly fathers, like my dad, cannot begin to compare to the greatness of our Father. He loves you so much! He is perfect in all of His ways! He provided the way for you to know Him intimately forever. Jesus is preparing His house for your imminent arrival. He treasures you and wants the very best for you. He sent His Son to reveal His heart for humanity. Embrace this love! Trust our Father! Ask Him for what you need. Talk to Him. Cry out to Him. Sing to Him. Walk all the days of your life with Him. There is no greater life than the one lived together with God alongside your brothers and sisters.

I want to share with you some thoughts from my friend, Nick. Nick is beginning to truly believe that God is his Father and that he is God's son. This is how things changed for him.

Being a Christian is hard. There are obligations when I try to be a Christian. I should go to church this Wednesday and Sunday because it is what I am supposed to do to be saved. I should read my Bible because I feel overwhelmed and everything else I have tried has failed to calm my anxiety. I should give a dollar to this homeless man on the corner because the pastor said I should be more generous with my American money but I should walk fast because he is scary and might steal from me. I should pray before dinner tonight because well, I forgot yesterday. I should pray before bed too, but I am really tired from the long day I just had. I should smile at this guy ringing me up at Target, he needs someone to like him because he is probably depressed because, let's be honest, he works at Target; but I have so much going on in my life, I can't actually care about him. I shouldn't look at this girl that just walked into this coffee shop, but she is so cute. I just won't talk to her, but she just sat next to me and smiled; come on, stop looking! Being a Christian is really hard.

Why is it so hard? The pastor seems so joyful and carefree; how can he do all of these obligations and be so carefree? How can this guy love his wife so much, does he even notice the cute girl sitting in front of him? How can you say there is more to life when you have all the money in the world? How can these people in poverty have smiling faces when they are staving? How can this girl feel whole when she was abused as a child? How can you forgive him, he just killed your husband and your children's father? How could you have beaten this addiction? My dad can't? My sister can't? How can you feel so loved when you are in the same stage of life as me and I feel utterly alone?

Being a Christian is hard. But being a Son is easy. Being a Christian has obligations, but being a Son doesn't; being a Son has inspiration, love, obedience, awe, desire, and a very light yoke. We can pull any noun Jesus uses to describe what we are to Him, what we should be in this faith: sheep, children, followers, servants, and disciples. All of these at their core have nothing to do with obligation to being a better person for no reason, just to be a Son to the one and only God. I put so much pressure on myself on being a Christian I forget to be a Son. When I am a Son, I will go to church, not to be saved, but to be with my family. When I am a Son, I will read my Bible, not to try and fix myself, but to learn more about my Father, the Father that created me. When I am a Son, I will give money to the homeless man, not because I heard one time I should, but

91

because being generous opens opportunities to show our Father's love to anyone receiving it. When I am a Son, I will pray for my food, not because I should, but because my Father has provided me with the food to live this life, just to His Son, nothing else. When I am a Son, I will pray at night, not to make up for all of the lost time I didn't at work, but because my Father wants to talk with me and be with me. When I am a Son, I will smile at the person at Target, not because he needs someone to like him, but because my Father loves him just as much as He loves me, and the Target guy deserves to know. When I am a Son, I won't look at the girl in the coffee shop like an object, but I will look at her like my Father does, a beautiful daughter He has created, and she deserves the upmost respect, and if she doesn't know she has a Father that loves her, she deserves to know.

Being a Christian is hard, but with God, everything becomes easy, light, simple, carefree, whole, joyful, and full of life. Jesus has shown us how to be a Son; the answer is with Him.

The Weight of Getting Love Right

> The glory that you have given me I have given to them, that they may be one even as we are one, I in them and you in me, that they may become perfectly one, so that the world may know that you sent me and **loved them even as you loved me**. (John 17:22-23)

Think about this scenario for a moment. This prayer of Jesus that we find written in John 17 was prayed just before Jesus' arrest, trials, floggings, and death on a cross. Jesus knew the time was quickly approaching for His ultimate sacrifice. Who was so important to Jesus that, before this horrific event, He would take the time to pray? He prays for us, the family of God! He prays we would be "one," just like Jesus and the Father are one. Jesus desires wholeness within His family. He doesn't want division or fighting. He prays we would love each other, care for each other, get along with one another, and forgive one another.

Jesus explains why the family of God needs to be one as He and the Father are one when He prayed, "That they may become perfectly one, so that the world may know that you loved them even as you loved me." When the church gets love right, a watching world has a lens in which it can see the love our Father has for it. This is an amazing opportunity for the family of God!

This is what Amal perceived when she visited my church family at one of our gatherings. She wrote, in the report she turned in to the professor about her experience, that our church was like a family. She saw the oneness we have with one another and, although she didn't fully realize this when she visited that night, what she truly saw was God's love for her. When she witnessed my church family praying for one another, she saw God's love for her. When her meal was purchased for her, she experienced God's love for her. When she saw the closeness my family has for one another, she witnessed the love of the Father.

I love any opportunity that brings my friends who do not yet follow Jesus into contact with my church family, because I know they will see God's love displayed through our love for one another. I can't tell you how many times this has happened. People see the relationships my church family has and it is so foreign to them because of our westernized, individualistic culture. We share our possessions and belongings. We support and encourage one another. We help each other raise and look after our kids. When people see this kind of love crossing ethnic, gender, and economical lines, it screams, "God loves you!"

"Is this Heaven?" "No, it's Iowa."

My senior year of college, I was blessed with a free airline ticket within the continental United States. With spring break rapidly approaching, I could have flown to any one of the 48 states eligible for the voucher. I could have gone to any beach in Florida. I could have visited any city on the West Coast: Seattle, Los Angeles, or San Francisco. I could have flown to a national park like the Grand Canyon or Yellowstone.

When I told my friends where I was going with this free ticket, they were either shocked or disgusted. They would ask, "Why are you going to Des Moines, Iowa? There has to be some place better to go. Des Moines! Seriously?"

Here's the thing—I wasn't going to Des Moines to see the city of Des Moines. Although I've come to appreciate the capital of Iowa over the years, as a 21-year-old college student, I can promise you there was absolutely nothing about the city of Des Moines that made me want to go there for spring break. But it wasn't about the destination, it was about who was there. And who was there? My lovely fiancée, Gretchen Stafford, living with her family and preparing for us to get married. At that point, I hadn't seen her for three months. I couldn't wait to board a plane and touch down on the land of corn and pork, because the person I loved more than life itself lived amongst the corn and pork. It was the best spring break I ever had!

Jesus describes heaven as *my Father's house* in John 14. The vision we have of heaven from John in the book of Revelation is pretty spectacular. Heaven, in all of its grandeur, will be an amazing sight to behold. But I am not desirous to go there simply for the streets of gold and pearly gates. I am thrilled to go there because my heavenly Father's house is there, which means my Heavenly Father is there!

The house of our Father is also the home of our family, the church, those who have passed on from death to life. One day we will join them and be reunited forever and ever. This is an amazing hope! I long for the day to talk with my grandmothers that I never really knew. I can't wait to converse with the likes of Abraham, David, and Peter. I can't wait to see my sister Penny's smile once again and give her a gigantic hug. For all of eternity, the family of God will be together in our perfect Father's house. That is a future worth looking forward to, brothers and sisters.

Party Conversation

I recently turned 40 years old and I can hardly believe it. It seems impossible in one sense, but whenever I try to play basketball, I am reminded I am definitely not 25, either! My lovely wife threw me a Goodbye-To-Your-30's party the eve of my big day. She orchestrated yard games, a fire, some of my favorite bad-for-you foods, and, of course, those in Minnesota I am blessed to call brothers and sisters came.

At one point, I was standing off to the side speaking with my friends Moody and Melissa. I was so glad they came. I've known them now for several years. I first met them when I became a teammate of Moody in an adult basketball league. They have become special friends since then and it was my honor to officiate their wedding last year. Moody and Melissa are inquisitive about faith and are still trying to figure things out at this point.

As we were standing there looking out over the adults and kids who came to share my celebratory event, Moody asked me if the people present were *my church*. After pointing out a few of those there that were not a part of my church, I told Moody, "Everyone else here is a part of my church family." It felt so right to say that to him. I felt so blessed to do so as well. As Moody and Melissa celebrated my special day along with everyone else who was there, I pray they experienced the love of the Father that night. I pray one day they, too, enter God's family through faith in His Son. I pray that Moody, whose earthly father passed away when he was young, will gain a perfect Heavenly Father who loves him more than he can begin to comprehend. I pray one day we stand together again at another party. The location for that party will be in our Father's house, where there will be no more death, tears, heartache, and shame. We will look around at the saints and say, "Wow! What a family!"

Family of God

The One Thing {Dan}:

The church is the family of God. We are brothers and sisters with the same Heavenly Father. Some of us are spiritual fathers and mothers to younger saints in the faith, while being the sons and daughters to those fathers and mothers that are further along in the faith than we are.

My Dad

Upon realizing that his wife was pregnant, a close friend of mine recently said, "Nothing is as complicated as a son's relationship with his dad. It's the defining relationship that will form the rest of that boy's life."

When I was a kid, my dad knew everything. He was as infallible as the Pope, and wise as a sage. Dad's approval meant everything to me and I tried hard for that approval.

When I was a teenager, my dad was irrelevant. He didn't understand the angst of Nirvana, the appeal of a cigarette, the longing for acceptance, the crush of peer pressure. And yet, his approval still meant everything to me. Though I wanted his approval, I also resisted it; I pretended like I didn't care.

When I started my career, my dad was a goal. He did (actually still does) a lot in his life. I wondered if I would ever live up to his expectations, be able to support a family, pay the bills, provide a house, and lead people the way he seemed to do effortlessly.

A few years back, I began to realize that many of my standards, hopes, and expectations were based on assumptions I held about my dad, some of which weren't true. I had put my dad on a sort of pedestal. It was, admittedly, a very me-centered pedestal. I had invented a dad who looked down (on me, of course) from his seat of wisdom, making judgments about what I was doing. I can tell you two truths about my invented dad. First, he was nothing like my real dad. My real dad is not very judgmental.

He is actually very proud of me for no other reason than just being his offspring. Second, I used my made-up dad as a stand-in for God. God—the all-knowing, irrelevant, distant, eternally disappointed daddy with unmet expectations.

In both cases, I didn't really know the person about whom I was making assumptions. You might be thinking, "How could he not know his dad?" Well, for me anyway, there's a difference between living with someone and knowing someone. To know someone, you have to stop assuming and start seeking, asking, observing.

I think that it was important for me to get to know my dad, because I think the model I hold of him in my heart and mind influences the dad I am to my own kids.

We all eventually become just like our fathers and mothers, right? Perhaps it stands to reason that our spiritual kids will also be like us. So, if I am to be someone's spiritual father, I'd rather model myself after my real dad than the made-up one. I'd rather fashion my life after seeking the real God than my eternally disappointed daddy god. If not, I think I might screw up the kids.

I don't want to screw up the kids. So I wrote a little set of steps to keep in my mind as I go about spiritually daddy-ing people.

1. Divorce my model of God from any assumptions I have made about my own parents.
2. Base my model of God on what I know to be true of Him, rather than what I fear.
3. Be the parent to others that God is to me.

I think back to Scott's story of the church janitor. I think that janitor was more like the eternally disappointed daddy with unmet expectations than the loving sort. Imagine if Scott had met a janitor that was practicing godly church parenting. Who embraced him, lovingly showed him the right way to do it, and then, after a high-five, took him out for an ice cream sundae.

Okay, maybe that's farfetched, but you gotta admit, sundaes are pretty awesome.

The One Thing {Sarah}:

There is nothing more wonderful yet confusing to me than the image of a father. The word alone sends shivers down my spine and at the same time stirs up feelings so fast I begin to feel motion sickness from the unsteady sensations of joy and pain swirling around inside me.

The very first layer of my truest self is child. It is the core of my being and the identity I claimed with assurance before anything or anyone else could influence me. I am daughter and it is through that lens that I see the world.

My dad died of a heart attack nine years ago. At the time of his sudden death, I was a troubled and distant 22-year-old. There had been four straight years of fights, lies, anger, and separation leading up to the day his life ended. We never reconciled; we never forgave. I openly admit that I have a father complex. Truth is, though, his passing is just a part of the emotional puzzle, because I've always had a father complex. He never taught me how to engage with a dad who delighted in me and offered love unwaveringly.

Science has tried to break down the process of grieving into a simple step-by-step sequence humans can understand, but breaking down something as big as death into the five stages of grief can seem unattainable. I'm naturally a right-brained girl, which means, when placed in stressful situations like dealing with grief, my dominant hemisphere shuts down submitting its efficiency to its subordinate counterpart. With stress hormones rising, the left hemisphere steps into leadership, functioning with unrelenting order, check lists and structure. Death is without a doubt stressful, and my poor right brain became overwhelmed within seconds. All the feelings of loss and regret were too much. Memories and voices were too vivid. Thank God for the left hemisphere, who looks the five stages of grief in the eye and says, "We can do this."

We all know the five stages of grief, and some of us have personally lived them out: Denial, Anger, Bargaining, Depression, and Acceptance. Each stage takes a different amount of time depending on the person who's left behind and her relationship to the one who has passed on. Three scenarios have been proven to add anxiety when one is processing death:

1. Family ties
2. Unresolved conflict
3. Sudden, unexpected passing

The odds were not in my favor when I lost my father. Processing the five stages was an extremely painful journey for me.

My grieving process has reigned for far too long. I've been stuck like glue in different stages, trying to make peace using my own limited strength. I can say that after climbing up and falling back down again and again with Depression, Bargaining and Anger. I have finally, in the last two years, reached the stage of Acceptance and been able to forgive. This sacrifice of pride has resulted in an opportunity for me to reestablish the way in which I experience God. Being able to now view God as both a Mother and Father to my spirit has birthed freedom and acceptance that I have never before felt.

In this section, Jamie takes us on a verse-by-verse journey through the New Testament that leads to the very heart of Jesus. In each verse, we catch a glimpse of His radical message and the beautiful way we can all grow together if we simply restructure our relationship views as family.

One life-giving source that moves with and through each of us.

One teacher who came to show us exactly how we can relate to that source and other humans.

Many, many children who are still learning how to grow together and function as healthy brothers and sisters.

I wonder what it would look like if we offered each other more grace. What if we opened ourselves up to more tolerance—we are all just children who find it hard at times to share, be selfless, and behave kindly. We are little, messy children who have been reborn of the spirit of God and have been given the rights to call Him "Father." I've learned the hard way that to have a good father's love is to truly have it all.

Every day, I remind myself that the very best identity I've ever been given is daughter, and it is that belief that saves me over and over again. No matter what anyone else says, I am seen as a beautiful, wild, accepted and uninhabited daughter, just trying to live up to what Jesus has already attained on my behalf.

The One Thing {Gretchen}:

The church as the family of God, as Jamie talks about in this section, is one of those things that God has shown and taught me by experience long before I understood it from a biblical truth point of view. And now that the two are coming together, I am in awe of how good God's plan is, to not only offer us a relationship with Him, but that in doing so, He also welcomes us into a family.

I mentioned a little in my bio that my parents were first-generation Christians and how that has impacted my faith journey. But another little tidbit about my growing-up years is that I never lived near blood family. We were not estranged to my relatives, but we were not in close proximity to them either.

In 1981, my parents moved our family from Greensburg, Pennsylvania, to Altoona, Iowa, sight unseen…kind of strange. We had no connection to Iowa, except for a family, the Hixsons, who were good friends from our church in Pennsylvania and who now lived in Iowa. I was only five, so I don't know everything that went into the decision to move, but I know the Hixsons encouraged my dad to attend a Bible college in Iowa, and my dad and mom decided that was a good idea, so off we went. But it didn't stop there. The place we were going to be renting wasn't ready yet. So, the Hixson family of five, who lived in a 3-bedroom, 1-bathroom house, welcomed our family of 4 (no Baby Emily yet) into their home. We lived with them for about a month while our house was getting fixed up. Again, I was only 5, so I don't know the half of what they did to help my family get settled, but I know they helped my mom and dad find jobs, they helped get my sister Leah and me enrolled in school, and they introduced and brought us into the life of their new church family in Iowa. They sacrificed their time, their convenience, their resources, and who knows what else, to make our family feel at home. They were, and continue to be, family to my family—they modeled the heart of Jesus by literally giving us a seat at their dinner table and a place to lay our heads at night. Family does that—it gives and sacrifices. It is inconvenienced, but the reward is deep: a long-lasting relationship and a place to know you belong.

Fast forward and once again, apart from a brief stint when Jamie's sister Penny lived in Pennsylvania after we were just married, we have never lived by family. Jamie and I love our families, and anyone who knows us could tell you that, but since we do not live by them, we have learned to rely heavily on the family of God for our daily needs. I would not have survived living 1,200 miles away from home as a young wife and mother without the spiritual moms, dads, sisters, and brothers that God gave us in Pennsylvania. These people became so dear to us, we even began celebrating "Friends Christmas" and "Friends Thanksgiving." Family does that, too. They celebrate life's triumphs and are there when life doesn't feel much like a celebration. When we moved to Minnesota in 2004, one of my biggest fears was that we were leaving all that "family" behind—that especially my girls were going to miss out on all those connections. This is what I mean when I say God taught me by experience, before I understood it in my mind. I still, after all that time, did not fully comprehend or trust that this was God's beautiful plan for His church. But it was, and in addition to our earthly family in Iowa and Ohio, and now those who had become our Pennsylvania family, God was preparing for us a Minnesota family, and to this day our family continues to grow and to grow.

The light bulb to connect my experiences to truth came on for me about two years ago. I was very distraught about some young girls who had been coming to our home and who had expressed to my daughter how sad they were that their family was incomplete. Specifically, they had no dad in their lives. I was washing the dishes and crying and wondering how in the world could I fix this one. As I lamented to Jamie, he recounted to me God's plan for His church—God wanted to be a Father to these girls, and on top of that, He wanted to welcome them into His family, "the largest family on earth," the church. God and His church were the answer to their incompleteness and this is the absolute truth. And what really drove the point home was when Jamie reminded me of how this truth had played out in my own family, in my own experiences. My mom, who was raised by a single mom and never knew her dad, came into relationship with a Heavenly Father. My parents, not living close to their earthly family, were brought into a spiritual family where they were encouraged, mentored, and supported as they raised us in the way of Jesus. My family and I, as we have pursued the call of God in our lives, again away from the earthly family that we love, have seen God multiply our "family" far beyond what could ever have been produced by only earthly means. In fact, there is a verse that someone told me a long time ago, when I first moved away from my mom and dad to begin my life with Jamie. It says, "And everyone who has left houses or brothers or sisters or father or mother or children or lands, for my name's sake, will receive a hundredfold and will inherit eternal life" (Matthew 19:29). I have experienced the fulfillment of this promise since the very first days of my life. God is always so good to us, but sometimes He lavishes His goodness on us—and the family of God would be one of those things.

The One Thing {Scott}:

I like Nick. I mean, I like Jamie, Gretchen, Sarah, and Dan, too, of course. But from my perspective, they make being Christian seem easy. At least Nick points out that it's really pretty hard. To become one, to be one, or perhaps more aptly, to live as one of God's children, is not an undertaking for the weak at heart. Any yahoo can tell you that church is family. I am by no means suggesting that Jamie is a yahoo. Nor am I saying that all churches are families, for there are many church buildings filled with souls attending only through guilt, obligation, or force of habit. But if you have an open and engaging personality of any depth, you might actually say that you have several families, with church being just one of the many.

Your spouse and children, parents, brothers and sisters, first and foremost, are your "real" family, but it wouldn't be thought of as unusual to consider your close friends as family, too. Colleagues at work can fall into that category as well. Beyond a blood connection, all are tied by a certain level of common intersests and goals, with varying degrees of love or affection, respect, and trust.

So what makes a church family different?

I consider my daughter's soccer team a family. But every season, a few players leave for greener pastures—or fields, more accurately—and others join us as an opportunity for growth. We grieve for those lost (most of the time) and welcome the new into the fold. However, from my past experience, at some point in time the team disbands as the girls grow up, get driver's licenses, jobs, and develop other interests. The family drifts apart. And sadly, so it goes with friends on occasion. More distressing in this day and age is how often that "real" blood family is torn apart. The work family? Sometimes it breaks up slowly, and sometimes you simply just get kicked out the door.

As the saying goes, "In life, all good things must come to an end." What

I'm learning, though, as I've worked through these book sections (and this one in particular) is that a family bound through church and faith, with recognition that Jesus is God's Son, and heaven is God's house, will never end. Eternal life is there for those that believe, and live, as God's children. The joy that Jamie has in his church family is evident in all his writing. And to have that same joy is something I wish I could find. But, as Nick described, wanting and achieving are two very different realities.

It's not as though I came into this book thing to become a Christian, and at times I've joked with the others that part of Jamie's mission for the project is to "save Scott." To be clear, Jamie approached me as someone he knew would say what he thought with a view from outside the church and be less concerned about what others said or thought about me. To be honest, I thought (hoped?) this book effort might help me in what I've perceived to be a search for faith. You, the reader, by now have probably found my search to be concerted at times and completely lackadaisical at others.

Patience is a virtue, or so I'm told. Unfortunately, it's not something I'm long on. But it's comforting to know that I'm working with others who've shown nothing but patience and understanding and—dare I say it?—love in regards to my thoughts on the subject of faith and family.

church
(noun) \\'chərch\\:

4. spiritual house

According to www.colognecathedral.net, on August 15, 1248, Archbishop Konrad von Hochstaden laid the first foundational stone for what we now know as the Cologne Cathedral in Cologne, Germany. In 1265, portions of the building had advanced far enough toward completion that services could be held there. But the cathedral was still a long way from being finished.

Although the cathedral was consecrated on September 27, 1322, the architectural work continued. It wasn't until 1506 that the stained glass windows were inserted; in 1560, work on the cathedral temporarily stopped. Well, *temporarily* probably isn't the best word to use here, because work did not resume until 263 years later in 1823.

The interior of the cathedral was completed in 1863, but the last stone wasn't placed on the southwest spire until October 15, 1880. From the first foundational stone being laid in 1248 until the last stone was placed in 1880, the total time of constructing this magnificent piece of architecture took 632 years and 2 months—or 230,741 days.

I've been to Cologne, Germany twice in my life and have seen this glorious Gothic cathedral during both visits. I've stood on the outside courtyard and gazed toward the top of the northern tower that crescendos into the sky. I've walked the choir loft and aisles in the interior of the building with wonder as I drank in each stained glass window portraying an ancient story. I've climbed the tower of the cathedral and looked out over the beautiful European city from the largest building height in the world until 1884.

For 632 years and 2 months, each individual stone was grafted into this splendid structure. Although the cathedral is in constant need of repair, the culmination of all these stones has become the most visually stunning creative structure man has made that my two eyes have ever seen.

The last night of my 2ⁿᵈ trip to Germany, Gretchen and I, along with my friends Eric, Lisa, and Rob, spent our final evening in Cologne. I'd been to the cathedral a few times during the day, but had never seen it under the stars. We checked into our hotel just before the sun began to set. After placing our luggage in the room, we decided to head out for a final meal in Europe before returning home to the United States the next day. The sun had set while we checked in, so by the time we walked back outside, the evening sky had given the city of Cologne its nighttime identity. I think my jaw literally dropped when I looked at the lit up cathedral in the distance. As extravagant as I thought the cathedral was during the day, it paled in comparison to the beauty of the cathedral at night. The lights on the outside of the cathedral illuminated the ancient structure with multiple shades of purple and blue. All five of us let out a collective "wow." To this day, one of my favorite pictures of all time is of the five of us that night with the gorgeous cathedral in the background.

When all of those thousands of stones used to construct the cathedral were fashioned together, the result became a grand and stupendous creation. But the house Jesus is building is far more majestic than the Cologne Cathedral. The house Jesus is building has been under construction for over 2,000 years now and the building will not cease until His return to this earth.

Spiritual House

In his first epistle, Peter describes the church as a *spiritual house,* with Jesus being the architect and builder:

> As you come to him, a living stone rejected by men but in the sight of God chosen and precious, you yourselves like living stones are being built up as a *spiritual house.* (1 Peter 2:4-5)

Long before Peter wrote these words, Jesus already told the disciples He was going to build His house. Peter was there when Jesus said so. Peter actually was the person Jesus was talking to specifically when He made the statement. In Matthew 16:18, Jesus told Peter:

> And I tell you, you are Peter, and on this rock I will build my church, and the gates of hell shall not prevail against it.

I will build my church. Humans throughout the course of history have built amazing architectural structures, such as cathedrals, temples, and skyscrapers. Although many of these buildings are creatively constructed and speak to the legacy of the architect, they will eventually become decayed and in need of restoration. These manmade buildings and houses are made of stones that will not last forever. Actually, the last time I was in Cologne, repairs to the Cologne Cathedral were underway. This is not true of the house Jesus is constructing, however! The house Jesus is building will never decay, die, or need to be replaced; the chief cornerstone in this house is the Son of the living God.

Peter's words found written for us in 1 Peter 2 are simply the words of Jesus from Matthew 18 expressed in a different manner. At this point in time, Peter had seen how terrific this *spiritual house* (the church) had become in just one generation. Peter, on the day of Pentecost, empowered by the Holy Spirit, spoke to a large crowd in Jerusalem about who Jesus is. When he finished speaking, Acts 2 tells us that those who heard the message were *cut to the heart* and asked, *What shall we do?* (Acts 2:37). We are told a few verses later that 3,000 people were baptized and added to their number that day (Acts 2:41).

From that time on, the spiritual house of Jesus has grown, expanded and become a remarkable house! When Peter wrote the 1st century church and told them they were being built into a spiritual house, he was reminding them of their identity. As a spiritual house, Peter told the early church they gave glory and honor to their architect and builder, Jesus Christ, the Son of the Living God!

Living Stones

> As you come to him, a living stone rejected by men but in the sight of God chosen and precious, you yourselves like *living stones* are being built up as a spiritual house. (1 Peter 2:4-5)

This weekend, I am in the Chicago area for my daughter Tori's club soccer team. Since the first games are not until Saturday morning, many of the families took the train into downtown Chicago on Friday night to see the sights. We explored Millennium Park and Nike Town on Michigan Avenue. We went to the beach just to touch Lake Michigan. Of course we went to the original Gino's East to eat way too much deep-dish pizza as well.

While we were walking down Michigan Avenue, my friend Scott (yes… the Scott writing in this book) said we should stop and look at the Tribune Tower. I walked over and was immediately intrigued by the unique design of the building. Scott began to point out some of the stones and I was amazed at what I saw. There are literally stones from famous landmarks around the world embedded into the tower. There is a stone from Yale University, Stockholm City Hall in Sweden, Pearl Harbor in Hawaii, Omaha Beach in France, the White House in Washington D.C., the Cathedral of Notre Dame in France, the Berlin Wall in Germany, the Tower of David in Jerusalem, the moon (yes—the moon!), the Alamo in Texas, the Coliseum in Rome, and of course, the Cologne Cathedral. I've only listed a tiny fraction of the stones from all over the world that are grafted into this amazing tower.

As I looked at the Tribune Tower and realized there were stones from all over the world used to help build it, I couldn't help but think of Jesus' spiritual house. Living stones from all over the world for the last 2,000 years have been grafted into Jesus' house. I've been blessed to meet some of these living stones. I know of living stones from all over the United States. I know living stones like Chisom from Nigeria, Alexandra from Peru, Jeff from Canada, Minh and Quyen from Vietnam, Sergio from El Salvador, Jorge from Mexico, and Ilya from Kazakhstan. Each of these stones is precious, living, and unique. Their uniqueness and wonder are magnified as they are grafted into Jesus' universal house. They join in the house where other living stones from the last 2,000 years are already in place. Biblical stones like Peter, James, John, Paul, Lydia, Silas, Timothy, Priscilla, and Aquila. There are early church father stones like Augustine, Ignatius, and Polycarp. And living stones after these church fathers like Luther, Edwards, Graham, and King.

All of these living stones give glory to the builder of the house. As the writer of Hebrews put it:

> For Jesus has been counted worthy of more glory than Moses—as much more glory as the builder of a house has more honor than the house itself. (Hebrews 3:3)

In today's HGTV world, we should get Hebrews 3:3 and understand the honor the builder of a house receives. You can turn on the HGTV station any time during the day or night and watch episodes of interior designers, carpenters, painters, or treehouse builders using their creative process to form something amazing out of either trash or nothing. And at the end of each episode, when they show the before and after pictures, we (the viewers) are astonished at what the builders created. The completed projects by these experts are awesome, but the creators of the projects receive all the glory.

Only Jesus can take dead stones that are formed uniquely, with jagged edges and misshaped ridges, and make them alive, useful, and able to be grafted into His spiritual house. When I look at this spiritual house and realize I am just one small stone amongst so many across the annals of time and the surface of the world, my heart and soul magnify the builder, my beloved Savior Jesus Christ.

Here's the thing about Jesus' house – Jesus made all of the individual stones in His house alive. Jesus made Paul a living stone. Jesus made Peter a living stone. Jesus made John a living stone. Jesus made Billy Graham a living stone. Do you get the picture? Because of this, I think we should be asking ourselves this question: "How do I become a living stone?" Well, the answer to that question is found in the opening phrase of our verse in 1 Peter 2:

As you come to Him, a living stone…(1 Peter 2:4)

The *Him* in this verse is actually Jesus. Jesus is the living stone! The only way to become a living stone is to come to THE Living Stone. And when we come to THE Living Stone, THE Living Stone breathes life into us and we become a living, breathing, and vibrant stone.

If you remember from the "Called Out Ones" section of this book, we looked at Genesis 2:

> Then the LORD God formed the man of dust from the ground…
> (Genesis 2:7a)

God formed Adam out of the dust, but he was lifeless. Adam wasn't walking, talking, singing, or working, because lifeless people don't do any of those things. It continues, however:

> …and (God) breathed into his nostrils the breath of life, and the man became a living creature. (Genesis 2:7b)

God breathed His breath into Adam and Adam became a living being.

What we sometimes forget is that Jesus is God and was present and participating in the creation of this world, which included Adam. John testified to this in the opening sentences of his Gospel:

> In the beginning was the Word, and the Word was with God, and the Word was God. He was in the beginning with God. All things were made through Him, and without Him was not any thing made that was made. In Him was life, and the life was the light of men. (John 1:1-4)

Jesus created Adam and then breathed the life that was in Him into Adam's soul. Jesus has the power to move someone from death to life—not just physically, but spiritually as well. When we come by faith to Jesus, the life-giving, life-breathing Living Stone, Jesus receives us and transforms us into a living stone ready to be placed into His spiritual house: the church.

One of my great joys is to watch human stones become alive through Jesus and then be placed into His house. Sergio is one of those stones. About two years ago, my friend Nate befriended Sergio through a self-defense/ martial arts club. Sergio was passionate about martial arts and the *energy* he sensed in people. He spoke openly about that energy with Nate the first few times they hung out together outside of the club. Sergio sensed Nate had a lot of energy and, through their friendship, Nate began to share with Sergio that this energy inside of him isn't really energy at all. This energy is actually a person and that person's name is Jesus! Sergio didn't know it yet, but he was witnessing Nate's true identity as a living stone that has been built into a spiritual house.

After a short while, Sergio was introduced to the rest of the living stones in my church community and I began to spend time with Sergio. The first few times we were together, we read the Gospel of John. Sergio would comment about how much he enjoyed being around my church. He sensed a love and respect for each other that he hadn't seen in other places.

Eventually Sergio came to Jesus and asked to receive the life Jesus offered him. Sergio trusted Jesus as his Lord and Savior and this stone known as Sergio had the life of God breathed into him. Sergio became a living stone! His desires immediately changed and he became increasingly hungry for God and His Word. It is captivating to watch the transformation inside of Sergio take place.

In May of 2014, I had the privilege to walk out into a chilly Lake Nokomis (lakes are still very much cold during the month of May in MN!) and baptize Sergio. His El Salvadorian blood became more chilled with every step farther from shore! When the lake's waters reached waist high, we turned around to face the beach. There we were, two living stones, out in the water looking back at several other stones. As Sergio sprung out of the water (and I mean sprung—he was very cold), he publicly identified himself with Christ and His church.

We walked back to the beach and each person hugged Sergio, wet shirt and all. There was a cause for celebration; this living stone publicly identified himself with Jesus and His spiritual house. In that moment, amongst the smiles and hugs, I, like the writer of Hebrews, praised Jesus, the builder of the church, for carrying out what He promised He would do. "To Jesus be all glory, honor, and praise!" Amen.

Spiritual House

The One Thing {Dan}:

For 632 years and 2 months, each individual stone was grafted into this splendid structure...

While in Ireland, I lived about 50 miles from the famous Blarney Stone. This stone, when kissed, is supposed to give the kisser the gift of gab, which is the ability to talk for hours on end. I kissed that stone 3 times and yes, I do talk a lot.

In order to kiss the stone, you have to get in line, slowly make your way past vendors selling Blarney-themed t-shirts, up a long staircase to the top of the Blarney Castle, and finally you get a coveted turn to place your puckered lips on the precious Blarney Stone. At first, the stone was just an ordinary, rough part of the wall of a castle. That was before it learned how to make people kiss it. Now, all that kissing has made it smooth, almost soft, sometimes moist—truly a stone to be remembered.

If you ask me what kind of living stone I want to be, I'll tell you the Blarney Stone every time. Imagine people lining up, even buying a t-shirt, to announce the fact that they kissed you! (I spent much of high school imagining this kind of scenario.) Imagine how valued, important, and worthy of prominent placement as a living stone in a good house you would feel!

Problem is, I bet most of us don't feel like the Blarney Stone. My desirability feels more akin to fill dirt. Fill dirt is the stuff that people put under other stuff that looks better. My neighbor used fill dirt to even out his yard and now adorns the spot with better looking stuff like plastic deer and lawn gnomes. That's how I feel much of the time. Put me under the lawn gnome.

I recently brought on a few people to assist with a work project. This morning, one of the less experienced folks said to me something along the lines of, "I see all that you guys are doing here and I'm just afraid I won't be good enough. I'm afraid I won't match up." I laughed and told her about imposter syndrome.

"Did you know that 5/8 of all the people here, from the CEO to the janitor, are afraid that their peers will discover they aren't good enough? That their hidden ineptitudes will be found out? The thing is, the same survival instinct that causes them to hide is what keeps them from growing. The less they grow, the more they have to hide. It's a tragic cycle, really."

Reading Jamie's chapter on Spiritual House made me realize that I personally struggle with imposter syndrome. Somehow, Jesus doesn't see me as fill dirt.

I ask myself how this can be. Doesn't Jesus have eyes? Doesn't Jesus see me for the imposter I truly am? Then I am reminded of another stone: granite.

A few years back, my wife and I purchased a granite countertop for our kitchen. I find granite's diverse hues and shades fascinating. When we picked our slab, I spent nearly an hour just looking at it in the sunlight. Each angle revealed some new gorgeous color or grain. Granite is formed when magma erupts from under the Earth's crust and travels toward the surface. Much of that magma doesn't ever see the light of day and cools very slowly, over the course of many thousands of years. During this process, it crystalizes and forms granite. Granite didn't start out beautiful. Time, heat, pressure, and lots of stressors made it beautiful. And, even after all that, a single piece of granite is only so great by itself. A house made of lots and lots of worn and polished stones? That's amazing.

Jesus sees me, not as I am right now, but He sees me outside of time. He sees me for all I will be over all of eternity. I might feel like a slab of fill dirt right now, but dang it, there's a granite slab in there somewhere. Jesus sees it in me. Jesus wants me in His house. I'm some kind of living stone, even if not the Blarney Stone. And even though I'm writing, this is not just about me. He sees the same in you, right? You are not fill dirt! You do not need to hide. You get to grow and learn and become the stone He wants for His house. Jesus already sees you as that stone. So much that He wants you in His house. Right now.

There's one more thing about imposter syndrome. When I counsel those that are feeling it, I tell them the quickest way through it is to pay attention to what they appreciate in others and then to pay compliments. This gets the attention off of one's own shortcomings and redirects it toward a positive goal. It also makes the work environment a lot more fun. Maybe we should do that to the other living stones around us. Praise that crazy German Berlin Wall stone! Compliment that Jewish Tower of David stone. Be kind to that loopy Moonstone. Give that defeated Alamo stone some love. You get my drift. I bet all of us stones feel like fill dirt from time to time. Let's get over the imposter syndrome, realize whom we are and are yet to be, and share some love.

Thanks, Jamie, you goofy Ohio Buckeye stone. This was a great chapter.

The One Thing {Sarah}:

Seven hundred years before Jesus was born, there lived an eccentric prophet named Isaiah. His visually engaging written work has been collected and celebrated throughout the generations. Isaiah was one of greatest hope spreaders and truth tellers of his time. Even today, his words are alive and moving. Isaiah was best known for his foretelling of a coming Messiah who would turn the tables on the rich and powerful and become the greatest advocate for the oppressed. The prophesied Messiah did come, just like Isaiah foretold. That Savior was a boy named Jesus.

Isaiah declared the same message Jamie has been inspired to write about, the same message Peter used to further the church after Jesus death. Three different eras, three different leaders, three different men, one unchanging idea. The straightforward concept of laying a single foundation stone before growing a structure is an example everyone can understand, but catching the metaphor for using one spirit before growing a faith takes some heart interaction. Isaiah 28:16 announces:

> Therefore thus says the Lord GOD, "Behold, I am the one who has laid as a foundation in Zion, a stone, a tested stone, a precious cornerstone, of a sure foundation."

This beautiful analogy can be found throughout the Bible, in both testaments. Spoken over and over again, affirming the truth.

A stone is a separated piece from a larger rock. Jesus, although He was a man, somehow also was the revelation of God. Like a stone is a piece of rock, so Jesus was a piece of God, yet God in fullness. I can't explain it, and I have yet to find someone who can. But regardless of the explanation, this mysterious belief is what our Christian faith is built upon, and this humble Jesus man is our living cornerstone.

We can read the Gospels and interact with both Jesus' endearing humanity and awe-inspiring divinity. We can read the words recorded by ordinary men who lived life alongside Jesus day by day, men who trusted the work of their Lord worthy enough to be recorded and remembered. When we read their writings, it doesn't take us long to catch on to the rebuilding work of Jesus. He was full of freedom and love, ready to use any castoff stone to develop, expand, and strengthen His kingdom.

A sure dishonor falls upon a church when the church itself is the one doing the rejecting of stones instead of building with them. I have been a part of four churches. Each one has been completely different from the one before. Each left its permanent mark upon me. As a young child, I was viewed as a living stone from the very day I was born—a valued part of the structure of our church. Even if my value was as simple as singing a quiet solo in front of the church on Sunday, they loved my childish heart and were blessed by my contribution, no matter how small. At the age of eleven, my parents met a conservative family, unlike any other I knew. My father was intrigued by their lifestyle, so much so that we soon left the only spiritual life I had ever known to begin attending church with them multiple times a week. Immediately, I was the rejected stone; rejected for being nothing more than whom my parents freely raised me to be. I was learning the rules and expectations of this new black-and-white system at a normal preteen pace and simply could not keep up. Rejected from my peers, who figured out how to survive under the radar better than I did. Rejected from siblings, who were once my playmates. Rejected from the leaders, who viewed me as trouble. After years of oppression, we finally left that church by the mercy of God alone. I was now sixteen. Five years doesn't sound like a long time, but the brainwashing left me questioning my value in every area of my small, sheltered world. As a family, we were left confused and directionless for a season, suffering from what I can only described as post-traumatic stress.

In the fall of my senior year, I entered in the back of a dark youth group room all alone and stood behind a sea of normal high school teenagers. They were engaging in worship that I never even knew existed. I felt the power and freedom right away. That night, after the group was over, I met two people who would change my life forever. They bent down low to scoop up my dusty, rejected, trampled upon stone of a self. They declared my value. They fought to bring me back to life. In that dark youth room that night, there was also a college freshman named Ben, who would become my husband. Ben and I stayed committed to the church that saved us for many years, until the spring of 2010, when Ben was offered an internship to utilize his shiny new degree in Biblical and Theological Studies with the Garden Communities. Ben and I decided to commit ourselves to the unfolding work of Jesus through the people of the GC. We are alive and connected, true living stones that are used every single day to continue building up a spiritual house of hope for all people.

The One Thing {Gretchen}:

I am not much of a builder. Legos and I were never friends; the pieces never seemed to fit right, especially the ones that were slanted or a different shape than the standard rectangular brick. So, in the end, I never created anything magnificent with Legos—normally just a square structure, with maybe a door and a window, and definitely not a roof—roofs were way above my Lego pay grade. So, in this section, I keep thinking about God as the Builder: how His perfect skill places each unique and living stone to create something amazing. The wonder of it all is magnified, because it is not just uniform rectangular bricks that He is building with, but one-of-a-kind people, each very different, but who each add something to the structure. The house is more complete than before they were a part. God has been doing this, as Jamie said, for over 2,000 years, and will continue to do it until it is done and every last stone that could be added has been added and has been set perfectly in its place.

We understand this on a small scale when we look at our families. Most people might find this shocking if they know our family, and I shudder to even speak it now, but there was a time after Tori and Isabelle were born that I thought maybe, just a passing thought really, that we should stop having kids after the two girls. I know, I know, it is an unbearable thought to think of life without the Mace, and thankfully we don't have to, but at the time, I thought our family was perfect as it was. What do I know? Well, now I know that God has given Jamie and me three beautiful and incredibly special daughters, and each one of them is an integral part of making our family complete. Tori brings passion and drive and a love of things beautiful; Isabelle adds carefree confidence and limitless creativity, and Macie brings affection, energy, and joy for life. They are the most magnificent things that I have ever had a part in creating (take that, Legos). If you were to take them out of the context of our family, I am doubtful they would be close friends—their interests, ages, and passions are all very different. I love that they are unique individuals, but if you want to see my heart burst open at the seams, you will take these three very unique creatures and then add Jamie and me (and we are pretty unique ourselves) and put us all together—

and I will be lost in the wonder of God's perfect plan. We are different, but we are the Miller family; God built our family together, and I love it, and I love Him more for it.

So, in the grander scale of the church, I am learning to trust the builder and embrace the uniqueness of myself and others as living stones being built into a spiritual house. Admittedly, with my daughters it is easy to appreciate their uniqueness and love them for whom they are and what they bring to our family. But in the church, those rare stones seem a little harder to fit into the structure. Sometimes I feel like the odd stone out and wonder where I fit in the grand scheme of things. I can find myself defaulting to my Lego thinking and wonder if it would be easier to build a church out of uniform rectangular bricks, or at least bricks that were shaped a little more like me. But, thankfully, I am not the builder. And just as God has perfectly constructed our family with each new member that has been added, He has masterfully built up together His church. One of the great joys of living in Minnesota has been the connections and partnerships we have been able to enjoy within our community and with other communities of faith. It is a good thing to meet living stones from different generations, different nations, different denominations, and to know that to the outside observer we may not seem to have much in common. We may not even think we have much in common at first glance, but the builder knows. He knows each stone and how it is needed to complete His spiritual house. And He will not stop building until every stone has been laid in its place. The more different stones, the better, because His finished spiritual house will have character and dimension and depth and variety, and it will be like nothing that has ever been built before. I have to think that, as we give glory to the builder, His heart bursts, too, to see all His individual children coming together into one with his beloved son, Jesus, as the cornerstone.

The One Thing {Scott}:

I am just a stone.

I am a living stone by the simplest definition, because I walk, talk, and breathe.

But I have not yet risen to the Christian definition of a living stone, as I have not come to Jesus to receive the life He offers, and taken Him as my Lord and Savior.

I am just a stone. And right now, I'm pretty bummed out about it.

And feeling cynical.

And hypocritical.

And to be honest, a little stupid.

I also feel a bit envious.

And amazed.

And inspired.

By the living stones around me.

But I remain confused.

I've read back on all Jamie's words, and my responses. The logic, which is probably not the "just right" word when you're speaking of FAITH, is there. And the love of Jesus is clearly within those that I've shared these stories with. I feel it in them.

This current story...what a great analogy. Taking what appears to be random pieces/people, and binding them together into one spiritual house.

It all makes sense.

When you hear it yourself.

When you read it yourself.

But what about when you don't feel it within yourself?

Am I destined to be...

Just a stone?

church

(noun) \ˈchərch\:

5. bride of Christ

I must admit something to you the reader. I've procrastinated writing this section for some time now. To be perfectly honest with you, I've even gone back and forth on whether to even include this section in the book. The reason for this inner turmoil lies with the fact that when two people get married the husband is the dude and the wife is the pretty lady in the magnificent dress. If you are still struggling to put the pieces together, let me speak more clearly – I AM NOT A PRETTY WOMAN. I am not a woman at all actually. If I were, I doubt I would be pretty anyway. Therefore, when I married Gretchen, she was in the beautiful white dress, not me. She was the bride in this scenario and I was the overachieving and lucky groom.

Gretchen, like most women I speak with, has no problem identifying herself as the "bride of Christ." Most guys however, like me, cringe uncomfortably when discussing the mere thought of it. I don't blame my brothers for this. As I've mentioned, it is kind of weird for a man to ponder being a bride.

So I have a bit of a dilemma here. And if you are a part of the non-female gender then I guess you may have a problem as well. But I've found there is too much imagery in the identity of the church being the bride of Christ for me to ignore simply because I feel a bit creepy about the whole concept.

Betrothals, Marriages, and Feasts

Before we look at some text from Scriptures regarding the church being the bride of Christ I deem it necessary to immerse ourselves in some cultural wedding traditions of Jesus' day.

For us westerners the first aspect of marriages 2000 years ago may be difficult to digest. But the fact remains that most frequently marriages were arranged back in the day. Typically the groom would work out some kind of pact with the perspective bride's family. After both parties made an agreement, the future husband and wife would have a betrothal ceremony. Betrothals were similar to what we would know as being engaged. Yet betrothals were more binding by nature than the engagements of today. For all intensive purposes, when two people were betrothed to be married in Biblical times then it was more like they were married but living in separate places rather then being engaged. Think of it as being married but not allowed to enjoy the act of marriage between a husband and wife (hint, hint, wink, wink). Actually, under Jewish law, it was punishable by death if the woman had sex with another man during the betrothal period. If you remember from Luke's account of the birth of Jesus, Joseph (Jesus' earthly father) decided to put away Jesus' mother Mary privately to spare her the punishment of death after it was revealed she was pregnant. Thanks to a visit from an angel, Joseph was informed that the Holy Spirit conceived the baby in Mary's womb and this baby would indeed be the prophesized Messiah. Joseph ended up taking Mary to be his wife and the rest is history. In summary – betrothals were a pretty big deal!

Now back to the betrothal ceremony. During this ritual, under the official canopy, the man would pour out wine into a cup, drink it, and then offer a sip to the woman. This action was the husband's way of saying; " I am willing to lay down my life for you." The wife, by accepting the cup and drinking of the wine, was symbolically saying; "I promise to lay down my life for you."

After this observance, the husband would leave and go prepare a home for the couple to live in. When he was done building the home, he would return to the wife and let her know their place of residence was completed. Family and friends would gather for the Marriage Feast and celebrate the couple's new life together. Following the banquet, the couple would be led to a room where they would consummate the marriage. Then when all of this activity is completed the newly married couple would move in to their home and initiate a new joint life.

With this cultural information in mind, lets now look at some Scriptures to help us understand our identity as the bride of Christ.

What we Learn from a Best Man

John the Baptist is this unique guy in the narrative of Jesus. He's described as a man that lives in the wilderness, wears camel hair for clothes, and eats honey and locusts. I like honey and if you are an outdoors kind of person then living in the wilderness may not seem too weird. Eating locusts and sporting camel hair however is just plain different.

Scripture tells us that John the Baptist's main role to play in Jesus' story is to prepare the way for Him to come. John took this preparation responsibility very seriously! He told everyone who would listen and even those who didn't want to listen about this amazing person who was about to step on to the scene. John told them this promised Messiah, or savior, to come would be far greater than he could ever be. John went as far as saying that the sandals of this promised Messiah were too worthy for John to even untie. John prepared people faithfully each day for the coming Messiah. He accomplished this task by using words like "behold" and baptizing people in the Jordan River. Then one day the promised Messiah Jesus showed up. John then shifted his message from, "one day this guy is coming" to "Hey everyone! He is here." People started following Jesus, the promised person John the Baptist prepared people for. Although John's apprentices left him to follow Jesus, he rejoiced. Some of John's other followers didn't share in his generosity however. They began to grumble to John that many people were leaving John to follow and submit to the teachings of Jesus. Here is John's response in John 3 to the news of his deserters:

> You yourselves bear me witness, that I said, "I am not the Christ (Messiah) but have been sent before him." The one who has the bride is the bridegroom. The friend of the bridegroom, who stands and hears him, rejoices greatly at the bridegroom's voice. Therefore this joy of mine is now complete.

John's response helps us see a couple truths. First, when we ponder the Marriage Feast taking place after the betrothal period, Jesus is the bridegroom in this scenario! John understood that Jesus is the groom and those who choose to follow Him are His bride. John wasn't envious of this arrangement. He says the friend of the groom "rejoices greatly" because he knows the bride and groom are together. John's role, as the friend of the groom, was to prepare the way for the groom, not actually be the groom. What kind of best man would try to steal the bride away from the groom! John wasn't jealous of Jesus because he knew the roles he and Jesus play. John actually rejoiced because he knew how thrilled the bride and groom would be together.

John also said, "The one who has the bride is the bridegroom." The English word "has" fails to express the full measure of the Greek word John actually pronounced. The Greek word translated "has" in this sentence renders the understanding of "to be closely joined, to adhere or cling to, to possess" (credit to blueletterbible.org). John was saying Jesus is closely joined to and possessive of His bride, the church. He has a strong commitment to His people and He desires a strong commitment from the bride towards Him. Jesus loves His bride fiercely and is so full of joy like a groom on the day of the Marriage Feast.

Secondly, we learn that we, the church, are the bride of the groom Jesus. Jesus clings to us and he desires for us to cling to him as well. Remember the betrothal ceremony? When the bride drank from the cup offered to her by the bridegroom she was saying, "I will lay down my life for you."

We are not just guilelessly dating Jesus. The arrangement isn't designed for us to try out the relationship for a little while and then bail upon any inconvenience. We are in a committed, eternal relationship with the King of Kings and Lord of Lords. He loves us deeply and passionately and I am pretty certain He would be thrilled if we would love Him similarly!

I've been married to Gretchen now for almost 19 years. Our commitment to each other is intense! I would do absolutely anything for her and I am fairly certain she would do the same for me. There is no other relationship

I have from a human standpoint that begins to come close to my passionate love and pledge to her. Because of this, my mind is blown as I strive to fathom Jesus' covenant, as our groom, to the church, his bride. I know He loves us about a billion times more than I love Gretchen. Although I can't conceive how this is even possible I believe it to be true.

Jesus Really, Really Loves the Church

The English word "love" encapsulates so many layers of understanding and depth. I can say, "I love almond croissants" but I can also say, "I love my three daughters." On most days these sentences mean two different things (it is sometimes hard to imply sarcasm in writing).

When I was a young lad growing up in the west side of Columbus there was once a girl I thought I loved. And you know what, I probably did love her in an almond croissant kind of way. Like a croissant, this fair maiden was pretty to look at and I liked the way she smelled. My heart would beat really fast when I was around her in the same way my heart races before I taste an almond croissant that has been toasted perfectly on the outside while the inside remains moist and flaky. I guess the analogy breaks down when I think about how I actually never had the courage to truly share with my dream weaver my complete feelings. That never happens with almond croissants. I confidently partake in that goodness without hesitation.

Fast forward to a little over a decade of my life and I am no longer a young lad in Columbus. I am now a little bit more mature young lad living in northeast Pennsylvania. As a sophomore in college I become infatuated with another girl I thought was very pretty, smelled good, and caused my heart to race uncontrollably any time I was around her. Although it took a year before Gretchen actually felt the same way about me (minus the smell good part), we eventually began to date.

Looking back on our relationship now, I think I realistically had an almond croissant kind of love for her initially. I loved her a lot but I often thought about how I benefited from the relationship more than what Gretchen was getting out of the whole deal. Somewhere along the way, however, this almond croissant kind of love morphed into something much more complex and sacrificial on my part.

I've had many guys in a relationship at the almond croissant stage of love ask me, "How do you know when she is the one?" My usual response is, "If you don't know she is the one then she is not the one yet." I don't mean this person they are in a relationship with couldn't become the one but if you don't know, then you know. Know what I mean?

There was this mosaic shift inside of me for Gretchen at some point in my deepening love for her. All of the sudden I had this protective and willing to do whatever it took to make her happy kind of love inside of me. Without a doubt I knew I would give my life for her in an instant. I loved her not like an almond croissant, but in a sacrificial and completely unselfish form.

Paul told the husbands in the church of the city of Ephesus they should "love their wives as Christ loved the church." He then goes on to describe how Christ loved the church in Ephesians 5:25-27:

> Christ loved the church and gave himself up for her by the washing of water with the word, so that he might present the church to himself in splendor, without spot or wrinkle or any such thing, that she might be holy and without blemish.

The phrase "gave himself up for her" assists us in understanding the fervor of Jesus' love for us, His bride. According to the website www.blueletterbible.org the word "gave" means:

> "To give into the hands of another, to give over power."

In order for Jesus' to present us, his bride, *"in splendor, without spot or wrinkle or any such thing, that she may be holy and without blemish"* then He had to hand over all of the power He rightfully earned as Creator of the world into the hands of the Roman soldiers and ruling powers. He gave himself up to the soldiers *for* His bride. Jesus gave himself up so our spotted, wrinkled, and blemished marriage feast wedding dress could be washed clean through

His sacrificial death. The Jews didn't kill Jesus. The Roman soldiers didn't kill Jesus either. Jesus killed Jesus. Jesus gave up his power because He was the only one capable of releasing the power He possessed. He did this for you and me, the bride of Christ. He loves us more than we will ever fully understand.

In this same section of writing in Ephesians 5 we are told that Jesus "nourishes" and "cherishes" the church. Our friends at www.blueletterbible. org again help us understand what this means:

> "**Nourishes**" – To nourish up to maturity."

> "**Cherishes**" – To warm, keep warm. To cherish with tender love, to foster with tender care."

Jesus, as our loving groom, is providing for us exactly what we need so we can grow in maturity and become the people He knows we should and can become. I desire for my spouse to mature in all areas of her interests. For instance, she loves making pizzas and has become quite excellent at this skill over the years. I am willing to help her grow and mature as a chef however I can. If she wants a new pizza stone, I'll find a way to get it for her. If I must be forced to eat several slices of pizza bliss then I will sacrifice and do my part for her growth! I must admit this sometimes causes me to evaluate if this act on my part is true love or the almond croissant love.

This is Jesus' action towards us. He is tender while providing everything necessary for us to grow and mature into the bride He believes we actually are. And He does all of this perfectly because He is the perfect groom!

Deer Paneling & Jesus Return

Gretchen and I were engaged for almost 10 months and we rarely saw each other during this period of time. We decided that after our honeymoon we would move back to Pennsylvania so I could begin work on a master's degree. Three months before we were married I was in Pennsylvania for the wedding of one of my college friends, and since this would be the last time either one of us would be in Pennsylvania before we moved I took some of my down time during the wedding festivities to check out a few living options for us.

I looked at two apartments that weekend along with my sister Penny so she could offer her advice. If you remember from the "Called-Out Ones" section our first apartment ended up being what we affectionately called "The Cave."

When Gretchen asked me to describe The Cave to her before we moved to Pennsylvania I did my best to convey the general layout and dimensions. I even remembered the décor of the apartment which I think scored me some points with my soon-to-be wife. I told her our first home was in a basement of a house somewhat secluded away from other neighbors. I recounted the fireplace, bedroom, drop ceiling, cabinets, and carpet.

I will never forget what happened when a few short months later we pulled into the driveway of The Cave with our little moving truck containing all of the very few possessions we actually owned. I was extremely nervous for Gretchen to see the residence we had decided to make our newlywed pad for one year solely based on my opinion. Our precious landlords that lived upstairs, Lloyd and Donna, came out to greet us. They were very excited for us to move in. We quickly walked down the outside stairs and into the laundry room that contained the front door of our brand new home. We walked through the door and turned to the right so Gretchen could look at the bathroom I so adequately portrayed. She seemed pleased. So far so good for me!

But then we walked over the hump at the bottom of the house stairs that led to the basement and into the all in one living room/kitchen/dining room. Lloyd was talking about the kitchen and how the house was heated by coal as I noticed all Gretchen was doing was staring across the room to the paneling that contained pictures of mountains, deer, birds, and other various wildlife animals. Now to my defense, I did tell Gretchen the entire apartment was made up of paneling along the walls. What I didn't convey (or honestly remember) was that an entire wall in the room we would be hosting people was made up of a paneling motif fit only for Paul Bunyan, Davey Crockett, or our landlord Lloyd.

Gretchen, as she always is, was incredibly gracious with me. For three years we hosted many people in The Cave while all of the furniture faced away from the deer paneling.

If I lived in Jesus' time I would have taken my responsibility to prepare a place for my betrothed bride much more seriously. I spent a total of 90 minutes looking at 2 different apartments. I am certain Jesus' construction of our future dwelling place with him is being meticulously executed.

Jesus told His disciples in John 14 that he, like a bridegroom that was betrothed to a woman, would be preparing a dwelling place for His bride:

> "Let not your hearts be troubled. Believe in God; believe also in me. In my Father's house are many rooms. If it were not so, would I have told you that I go to prepare a place for you? And if I go and prepare a place for you, I will come again and will take you to myself, that where I am you may be also." (John 14:1-4)

Our bridegroom Jesus is currently preparing a place for His bride the church and one day He will come back. Why? So we can be with Him! This is kind of the point of our faith right? To be with Jesus! Please hear me – I believe Jesus is with us now. We do have a relationship with Him presently on this earth and I passionately strive to convince anyone that will listen to me of this truth. But one day, when He returns, our faith will become sight. Our eyes will behold the bridegroom when He returns to this earth to take us with Him. We will celebrate together at the Marriage Supper and what a party that will be!

In John's vision recorded for us in the book of Revelation he describes this Marriage Feast in Chapter 19:6-9:

> Then I heard what seemed to be the voice of a great multitude, like the roar of many waters and like the sound of mighty peals of thunder, crying out,

"Hallelujah!
For the Lord our God
the Almighty reigns;
Let us rejoice and exult
and give him the glory,
for the marriage of the Lamb has come,
and his Bride has made herself ready;
it was granted her to clothe herself
with fine linen, bright and pure"—
for the fine linen is the righteous deeds of the saints.

And the angel said to me, "Write this: Blessed are those who are invited to the marriage supper of the Lamb." And he said to me, "These are the true words of God."

Are We Ready?

Jesus has offered each of us the cup of wine at the betrothal ceremony and by doing so has willingly laid down His life for us, His bride. What I've found with people through my interactions with them is some are holding the cup deciding whether or not they want to accept this amazing relationship Jesus is offering them through His death and resurrection. Others have partaken from the cup and by doing so have committed to laying down their lives for the bridegroom. Yet they have forgotten about this commitment or have become distracted by other plans or agendas.

But I also know of many brothers and sisters in Christ that not only have accepted and drank from the betrothal cup of Jesus, they are actively laying down their lives for the bridegroom each and every day. They do this by caring for the things their bridegroom Jesus cares about. They are serving the poor and marginalized of society. They love their neighbors and their enemies. They are proclaiming Jesus' message of joy, hope, and salvation. They enjoy the presence of their groom Jesus each and every day. They do these things because they love Jesus and are excited about His eminent return. Although they are not certain when He will arrive and the Marriage

Supper will begin they desire to be primed for this amazing day. These saints inspire me to be ready for the return of Jesus and I want you to be ready too. Are you?

Bride of Christ

The One Thing {Dan}:

During this ritual, under the official canopy, the man would pour out wine into a cup, drink it, and then offer a sip to the woman. This action was the husband's way of saying, "I am willing to lay down my life for you." The wife, by accepting the cup and drinking of the wine, was symbolically saying, "I promise to lay down my life for you."

That is a beautiful picture. I start out with the best of intentions. Certainly, I desire to pour my life out for my wife, my kids, my family, and my friends. I think three things come between me and actually living out that picture.

1. Knowing how to love Jesus

In the past, I struggled with the concept of loving Jesus. I found it easy to be in awe of Him, easy to work to follow His lead, but I found it hard to say I loved Him and feel like I was being honest. This changed when I realized that love doesn't exist in a vacuum. Jamie's almond croissant love might be able to live in a vacuum, but Jesus' love can't. I'm no expert, but I think Jesus' love requires four things: a source of love, a conduit of love, the communication of love, and a recipient of love. Jesus is the source. I desire to be the conduit and communicator. And (I admit, it gets a bit circular here) Jesus is the recipient.

This leads me to ask what it would look like if I loved Jesus this way. In search of an answer, I came across Jesus saying, "Truly I tell you, whatever you did for one of the least of these brothers and sisters of mine, you did for me" (Matthew 25:40, NIV). With that in mind, I can love Jesus by loving the "least of these." Based on Jamie's chapter, I can do this by providing them with whatever they need to grow in maturity and become the people that they are meant to be.

2. Knowing how to love people

As I read my last sentence, it sounds arrogant. As if I should know who people should become. I suppose that is where communication comes in. If I love Jesus, I'll communicate with Him. I'll tell Him I love Him. I'll also tell Him about other stuff. Since having this thought, I've stopped calling my talks with Jesus "prayer." When I think of "prayer," I think of something I do before a meal, or just in the morning. I want to be more open with my communication. I want to communicate like I really love Jesus. For example, yesterday I thanked Jesus for a great sunset and warm weather as I grilled dinner. Before that, I thanked Him for my job as I drove in to work. I think my family is slowly getting used to these outbursts.

I mention all this because I believe that Jesus knows who people can become. If I talk to Him and ask Him who He wants people to be, maybe He'll talk back. Maybe He'll tell me when I meet "the least of these." Or, maybe He'll tell me I am the least of these. Either way, maybe He'll tell me how to love and serve and pour myself out for the least of these. And since He's Jesus, that doesn't seem so arrogant.

3. Knowing love

Thinking about this led me to another realization. For years I have walked around with an assumption that, just because I am a Christ follower, I know how to love. For much of my Christian life, I have practiced the almond croissant love, rather than the Jesus love. Jamie described almond croissant love perfectly: "I loved her a lot, but I often thought about how I benefited from the relationship more than what Gretchen was getting..."

Like many overconfident men, I'm realizing that I'm not all that great of a lover. I have generously spent time with people that validate me while avoiding those that don't. There is a time and place for being validated, I'm sure. But maybe there is never a time and place for avoiding people who need more than they give. Sounds like work though, doesn't it? After a long day, I want to stay away from people who can't get their acts together.

So, besides Jamie and Gretchen, I wonder who is doing all this sweet loving that he writes about? Jesus seemed to. I sometimes wonder if Jesus ever felt validated by people, of if He was constantly wishing humanity would just shut up for one second so He could have a nice chat with His father. Jesus is one example, but I've experienced more examples. Judging by the output of their lives, some of my non-Christian friends do love much better than I do.

As an example, in the past two weeks I've been inspired by a co-worker. She has demonstrated that a lover will ask how her team is doing, really care about what they say, and then come back a day later with follow-up thoughts, ideas, and even gifts, based on what they said. It's refreshing to be around her, to watch her lead her teams. I feel fortunate to get to apprentice love alongside her. This is just one of many examples I can think of in my life.

I hope it doesn't sound like I'm beating myself up about not loving as much as some other people. I'm not. I'm actually excited for a chance to evolve a bit, to learn to love better. This excitement has opened my eyes and helped me to see and learn from all the wine being poured out around me every day. I want to be that kind of wine glass: constantly and joyfully pouring and not resenting it.

I hope this chapter will be an impetus for some great growth in my life and some great wine pours in the near future.

The One Thing {Sarah}:

Thanks to good old Walter Disney, I, like all the other '90s kids under his influence, believed love and marriage to be a magical spell that filled up the empty spaces between a man and a woman. The classic romances always started with a simple act of care, which caused them to take special notice of one another. It followed by an awkward interaction that revealed their humanity and continued with endless infatuation and curiosity. I was convinced, as a child, that even I could handle this sequence of falling in love without a problem. This misunderstanding completely shattered the day my grandpa explained marriage to me by using the unromantic words choice love. He explained to me how, through genetics, it is in our very human makeup to love parents, children and siblings without them having to earn it. Family love just happens; even in tough families, it's there. But marriage love is a choice and much different from the love that we all grow up feeling and practicing every day in our childhood. Even if we are not given the freedom to choose whom we are going to marry, we are each given the choice of whether to love the one we are married to. This is our decision, inheritance, and birthright, given to us from the Divine, and most commonly identified as love.

Refusing Grandpa's wisdom, I stuck with Walt's love concoction well into my youth. I tested the formula on a handful of boys. I tried the caring gesture, awkward interaction and endless curiosity with them. These boys seemed to be down with the same Disney spell as me. Each boy was wonderful, but after a few months, the spell would evaporate into thin air and we would be faced with a choice that neither one of us wanted to make. That choice would always boil down to the same thing: each time, one of us needed to yield something to the other and we couldn't do it. I guess it would be appropriate to call this the point where one of us would "pour out the cup" for the other, and the other refused to do the same in return. This is where I would hear Grandpa's wisdom in my head and understand that the next step in our relationship would be the testing of whether we would choose to continue in love. I'm speaking for myself alone here, but love without mutual submission is not a game I ever want to enter the arena to play. I have seen this act to be so crucial that I honestly don't even know if love between two people is possible without submission. You pour out your life for me, and I pour out my life for you. In this choice interaction, trust is formed and love abides every single time. I'm not blaming the boys alone; I admit, I was (and still am) terrible at pouring myself out.

There was this one boy, though, whom I dated for a few months before we found ourselves in a situation that tested our ability and willingness to pour out for each other. Just like all the other experiences I had, I struggled to trust the choice part of our love and thought if one of us needed to pour out ourselves for the betterment of the other, something was wrong. So I continued my track record and broke up with him. Somehow, though, through our broken relationship, the desire to work on and solidify our love became stronger and stronger. I remember sitting beside him in the cool summer grass under a canopy of stars when he asked me to give us a try again. I said yes, after agreeing that this time we would trust the choice love all the way to the point of pouring out and beyond. We wanted to do that for each other. We wanted to be that person for each other, even if it meant choosing day after day the practice of mutual submission.

If we, the church, are the bride, the cup has already been poured out before us. Because of this selfless act, we become the chosen ones, the ones being pursued, the ones invited into partnership. Now the cup has been handed over to us, leaving the choice love to be all ours. If we refuse to practice the act of pouring out, we will continue to find ourselves in broken relationships and churches full of discord.

This summer, I will celebrate my 10-year anniversary to the same boy I mentioned above. I have lived life with him long enough to say that the act of pouring out for one another is far better than any Disney spell. I trust him enough to pour out myself, and not a day goes by where he doesn't do the same for me. I get lost in the wonder of what a church full of trust and submission would look like. I truly believe that the more the church pours out in trust, the more will be poured out for the church.

The One Thing {Gretchen}:

The proverbial "they" say it is all about the dress when it comes to your wedding day. I tried to google who the "they" originally was, but all that popped up was a long list of bridal stores with that name and a book by Randy Fenoli. Randy is the wedding dress guru who became famous for masterfully finding girls "the one" on his show *Say Yes to The Dress*. In the promo for Randy's book, it reads: "Every bride wants to feel beautiful and wants to have her dress express the essence of who she is." I tend to think this statement is mostly true when it comes to girls and their wedding dresses, as it rang fairly true for me. I found my wedding dress in a magazine. The moment I saw it, I knew it was the one I wanted. I told my mom the dress just looked like me, and she agreed; I never even went to try on another dress. Instead, I hoped it was in my budget and called around to the local dress shops to see if anyone carried my perfect dress so I could try it on. Unfortunately, nobody had it in stock, but it was in my budget, so my parents allowed me to order it in blind faith, believing I would love it as much as I did when I saw it in the picture, and I did. The day of my wedding, as I put on that dress, I felt confident and beautiful and ready to be presented by my dad to my groom. And maybe it was the dress, or maybe Jamie was envisioning me as an almond croissant, but as I walked down the aisle toward him, all I saw in his eyes was overwhelming love, and I was excited to start our happily ever after.

In reading this section on the bride of Christ, Jamie is right, I don't have any trouble imagining myself as the bride. I cherish that imagery and get lost in magical wonder at the thought of Jesus being the one standing smitten as He waits for me at the end of the long aisle. But the part that got me this time was the dress. I couldn't imagine showing up at my wedding with a spotted, wrinkled, and blemished dress. I would not have walked toward Jamie with confidence or felt like I was anything even close to beautiful; I would have been embarrassed and ashamed and probably wouldn't have come down the aisle at all. So, it magnifies to me the love of Jesus that a spotted, wrinkled, and blemished dress was all I had to offer— all any of us has to offer. That was the essence of what we were. And then, to think, in a Cinderella moment on steroids, Jesus enters, our groom. We stand spotted, wrinkled, and blemished, but by His blood sacrifice, He presents us "to himself in splendor, without spot or wrinkle or any such thing, that she might be holy and without blemish" (Ephesians 5:27). That is some kind of love and that is some kind of love story. The invitation Jesus offers to be His bride is the opportunity to cover and change everything ugly in me and to walk confidently toward Him in pure and beautiful radiance to the adventure of life together. Who wouldn't want to say yes to that dress?

And so, whoever "they" are, they got it right. It really is all about the dress. And the dress freely given to me by Jesus makes me confident, excited, and ready to walk toward Him into the greatest happily ever after ever known.

The One Thing {Scott}:

I'm pretty sure it's hard to be the "Bride of Christ" when you're just dating.

And while dating in this current day and age is far different from when I was actually in the game, which is also vastly different from when Jesus walked this earth, the concept is still basically the same: meet, through happenstance or introduction by others; experience that little "click" that says, "I think I need to check this out some more;" spend some time together getting to know each other and see where it goes.

Sometimes it goes nowhere, FAST. Sometimes it goes nowhere, oh so painfully SLOW. Sometimes it hits you like a brick—I'm now thinking of my dear (though never met) friend, Charles the Plumber. But most of the time, it takes some time. As it did in the great love story of Gretchen and Jamie, commitment comes in a variety of shapes, sizes, and schedules.

What is Jamie's message in this Bride of Christ section? What is the ONE THING I'm supposed to find? I think it's this: Don't bail. Commit. Give it your all. To yourself, your spouse, your family, your friends, the church, Jesus.

But Jesus, that's a lot.

I don't know who is more frustrated: me or my fellow writers. They have shown unending patience, understanding, and care as I've shared my questions, concerns, and fears over these months together. As I noted before, commitment comes in many forms, but I also know that commitment is not easy to give or, on occasion, receive. When it's there, however, it is truly precious. Jamie's, Gretchen's, Sarah's, and Dan's commitment to me is truly precious.

I particularly like how Jamie put it to the guys asking him about determining "the one." He says, simply, "If you don't know, then you know." Thankfully, he throws in the saving clause…"yet." Because, as our readers have all come to see, I'm the "don't know…yet" guy.

I have been from the start, and remain so today. At least as of the day I write these words.

I'm kind of old school. None of this Match.com or Tinder stuff for me. I've gotten past the introduction, felt the "click," and continue down the "checking this out" path. I know I'm not in it alone, and that there are many others still holding the cup, searching for the sign that says, "Drink up." It's turning out to be more work than I thought it would be, but I'm good with that. I've got friends who will back me up anytime. And, like the story of the footprints in the sand, I'm pretty sure there's someone walking beside me along this journey.

Have I been carried at times? I think so.

One question for Jamie: Rather than subject Gretchen to three years of hostess-angst misery in The Cave, why didn't you just take down the lousy wildlife pictures? For crying out loud, she let you pick the home, sight unseen. That is truly a demonstration of her commitment and sacrifice. You are a wise and wonderful man, my friend, but every once in a while, you exhibit the true doofus nature of all Ohio State Buckeye fans.

The Epilogue:

Several weeks have passed since the last section of the book was completed. Why the delay in writing an epilogue? Honestly, I feel the pressure to consummate the thoughts found in this book into some kind of stimulating finish that leaves you, the reader, with awe and wonder. I realized today, however, that this would contradict the intention of why I sensed God pushing me to write in the first place.

If you remember from the introduction, all I set out to do in these pages was define, using God's inspired words of Scripture, who the church is. Instead of leaving you with awe and wonder after each section, I preferred to challenge you to think critically about how you view the church. My wonderful friends and co-authors did just that. They read each section and thought seriously about what the truths from God's words concerning the church meant, both for them and the people they follow Jesus with. Because I know these amazing people personally and met with them to discuss their responses to each section, I perceived their subtle transformation in thoughts and actions over the entire experience.

My hope for you, the reader, is to imitate what the responders have done. Would you please think critically about what it means for you and your church community to live as called out people, the body of Christ, the family of God, living stones being built into a spiritual house, and the bride of Christ? That is who you are! Why not operate out of those wonderful identities?

In these final few pages, I desire to turn the tables on my friends and respond to their writings. I have learned much from their reflections as well and will share those thoughts with the authors here. You are invited to follow along as well.

Dan

I've known you now for over 10 years and to describe our relationship by only using the word "friend" seems so inadequate. You are a brother to me. And I'm not just saying that because I am obligated to due to my writings in the "Family of God" section! Yet even in the midst of the closeness of this brotherhood we share, I still learned a few things as a result of your contributions to this project.

I discovered you have a man crush on the Marlboro Man, you have an affinity for fill dirt, and I'll cherish the visual you gave me of a young Dan Halvorsen in a purple sweat suit. But what I truly appreciate about you is your honesty and longing for transformation. Anyone that reads your responses knows exactly where you are presently with your thinking and actions, but they will also visualize, because of your heart's desires poured out on the pages, where you thirst to be. You are satisfied with nothing less than Christ-likeness in every aspect of your life. I love that about you and know you've exhorted me to do the same!

It's an honor to lead our church family together with you and I trust God continues to use you to help our people believe in the identity of who they are as a church, so we can be the people of God in the world we dwell.

Sarah

There's no record that I can find of Jesus practicing anything that disables His followers. I believe His goal through the church is to empower us to continue His work.

Of everything I read of your contributions to this project, these two sentences summarized to me what I've been enlightened to the most from you, Sarah. Because we share the same church family, I know this passion of yours personally. I believe with all my heart this is what Jesus wants, too. You know that Jesus truly yearns for His people, the church, to remove the man-made shackles that hinder us and to be unleashed to use our unique passions and abilities as we become all that we've been created by God to be.

I see you as a modern-day Moses, standing on the edge of the Red Sea, aggressively thrusting your staff into the water. As the waters part, you urge those behind you to walk with you on dry ground to the other side of the sea and into liberation.

Because of you, my friend, I can say with confidence that our little tribe of Jesus followers does not say to our people, "This is who we are and we need you to fit in and fill our needs." Rather, we say, "Who are you? What are your passions, desires, talents, and abilities? How can we come behind you and—through the power of Jesus, the training of leadership, and the encouragement from the saints—assist you in becoming all God made you to be for the glory of His name?"

Gretchen

Where do I start with you? Since we are approaching 19 years of marriage, it is extremely difficult to separate the thoughts you've submitted for this book with who you are to me—my wife, best friend, and greatest ally in the Kingdom of God. Yet you never cease to amaze me. Everyday I live I see the best of Jesus in you. No one I know exhibits the compassion, mercy, and drive of Jesus like you do!

This quote of yours from the "Body of Christ" section summarizes what I've learned from you so well:

I do not want to cut off, isolate, or shame parts of the body that are hurting, broken, or just fearful. I want to aid in healing, restoration, confidence, and growth. I really do need you, and you really do need me. And we all really, really need Jesus. I love that this is how He designed it to be.

I, too, have the tendency to be like Marlboro Man Dan. Although it can be easier and less complicated at times to go it alone, it is far less fulfilling and much, much less Christ honoring. God never gave up on us! Since the time of Adam and Eve's sin until now, He has always left a bridge of reconciliation if we, as mankind, are willing to make that walk across the divide. You, my love, believe this about everyone. You never give up on people and always believe the best in them. I've grown in this area because of you and am so thankful you've smoothed out quite a few rough edges to my faith and personality!

Scott

When we sat down together last year and I proposed the idea of you contributing to this project, you responded with a guarded enthusiasm. I understood exactly your reservations, but I knew your insights would serve as a meaningful perspective to this book. You greatly exceeded my expectations and I know the readers of this book walked alongside your journey with vested interest.

Of everything I read from the other contributors or what I personally wrote about in this book, no one took me on such a ride of emotions as you, my friend. Thank you for your willingness to open up your heart and let us in.

As I reflect on the words and ideas you penned, I am reminded of something. Although you are still evaluating and figuring out your beliefs on faith and God, I know how God thinks about you. God loves you, Scott, and He is okay with your questions. I know (and now the readers know) that your natural writing style is that of poetry. I say this because many of the 150 Psalms (book of poems) we have in Scripture are filled with the author's questions for God. I forgot that it is okay to be honest with God and ask Him questions. Thanks for reminding me of this. Keep asking those questions, my friend. I believe as you ask them together with your church friends, you will discover the truth. And as Jesus said, "The truth will set you free" (John 8:32).

In Closing

What you don't know about the process of writing this book are the precious times we gathered together as contributors to read our sections to one another. In those moments, we learned and grew from one another. We functioned like a family and Jesus was central to our conversations. We laughed often and shed tears at times. On any given night, one of us would take turns expressing our confusion over some form of theology and then the rest of us would lovingly help that person along. This experience has given me a little taste of what the church can and should be all about. In many ways, our group embodied the identity of the church we wrote about and I will be forever grateful for it.

In closing, I want to share a quote from Timothy Keller's book, The Prodigal God:

> Christians commonly say they want a relationship with Jesus, they want to "get to know Jesus better." You will never be able to do that by yourself. You must be deeply involved in the church, in Christian community, with strong relationships of love and accountability. Only if you are part of a community of believers seeking to resemble, serve, and love Jesus will you ever get to know him and grow into his likeness.

When it comes right down to it, the whole point of the church is simply Jesus! Through our interactions and sharing of life with the church—the people of God—we gain Jesus! Friends, Jesus is worth obtaining!

I hope the words of this book by my friends and I have assisted you in your journey toward and with Jesus. I pray you learn to know Him more deeply as you dive more fully into the relationships you have with those called-out brothers and sisters. I believe the greater we learn to love each other, the more we access of Jesus and we lift and honor Him to His rightful place.

Now to him who is able to do far more abundantly than all that we ask or think, according to the power at work within us, to him be glory in the church and in Christ Jesus throughout all generations, forever and ever. Amen. (Ephesians 3:20-21)

(from left to right: Sarah Stadler, Scott Clements, Dan Halvorsen, Jamie Miller, and Gretchen Miller)

Thank you for reading our thoughts on and hopes for the church. We pray the investment you made produces in you a greater love for God and his people.

Further resources, including the Being Church podcast, are available at:

www.consumedministries.com/beingchurch